MW01078053

MEGA

Early Childhood Education (064)

Part 2 of 2

SECRETS

Study Guide

Your Key to Exam Success

MEGA Test Review for the
Missouri Educator Gateway Assessments

Dear Future Exam Success Story:

First of all, **THANK YOU** for purchasing Mometrix study materials!

Second, congratulations! You are one of the few determined test-takers who are committed to doing whatever it takes to excel on your exam. **You have come to the right place.** We developed these study materials with one goal in mind: to deliver you the information you need in a format that's concise and easy to use.

In addition to optimizing your guide for the content of the test, we've outlined our recommended steps for breaking down the preparation process into small, attainable goals so you can make sure you stay on track.

We've also analyzed the entire test-taking process, identifying the most common pitfalls and showing how you can overcome them and be ready for any curveball the test throws you.

Standardized testing is one of the biggest obstacles on your road to success, which only increases the importance of doing well in the high-pressure, high-stakes environment of test day. Your results on this test could have a significant impact on your future, and this guide provides the information and practical advice to help you achieve your full potential on test day.

Your success is our success

We would love to hear from you! If you would like to share the story of your exam success or if you have any questions or comments in regard to our products, please contact us at **800-673-8175** or **support@mometrix.com**.

Thanks again for your business and we wish you continued success!

Sincerely,
The Mometrix Test Preparation Team

Need more help? Check out our flashcards at: http://MometrixFlashcards.com/MEGA

Written and edited by the Mometrix Exam Secrets Test Prep Team
Printed in the United States of America

TABLE OF CONTENTS

Learning Across the Curriculum

Problem Solving Skills

Being able to solve problems is fundamental to all other components of mathematics. Children learn the concept that a question can have more than one answer and a problem can have more than one solution by participating in problem solving activities. To solve problems, a child must be able to explore a problem, a situation, or a subject; think through the problem, situation, or subject; and use logical reasoning. These abilities are needed to not only solve routine/everyday problems, but also novel/unusual ones. Using problem solving skills not only helps children think mathematically, but also promotes their language development and their social skills when they work together. Children are naturally curious about how to solve everyday problems. Adults can take advantage of this inherent curiosity by discussing everyday challenges, asking children to propose ways to solve them, and asking them to explain how they arrived at their solutions. Adults can also invite children to propose problems and ask questions about them. This helps them learn to analyze different types of problems and realize that many problems have multiple possible solutions.

Common Steps That Prepare Children to Learn Math

The process of solving problems often involves the following steps: understanding the problem; coming up with a plan to solve the problem; putting that plan into action; and, finally, observing the outcome and reflecting on whether the solution was effective, and whether the answer arrived at makes sense. Solving problems not only involves learning this series of steps, but also requires children to develop the qualities needed to solve problems. Children who are able to solve problems have a number of characteristics. For example, children who are effective problem solvers are able to focus their attention on the problem and its individual component parts. They can formulate hypotheses about the problem/situation, and then test them for veracity. They are willing to take risks within reason. They are persistent if they do not solve a problem right away, and do not give up if their first attempt at solving a problem is unsuccessful. They maintain flexibility, and experiment with alternate methods. They also demonstrate self-regulation skills.

Using Problem Solving Skills in Daily Life

Young children continually explore their environments to unravel mysteries about how things work. For example, preschoolers use math concepts to understand that they have three toys, to comprehend that three fingers equals three toys, or to understand that two cookies plus one more equals three cookies. To do abstract mathematics in the future, young children will need two major skills that are also used to solve problems: being able to visualize a scenario, and being able to apply common sense thinking. Thinking and planning to achieve goals within the constraints of the properties of the surrounding environment is a natural behavior for young children. They will persist in their efforts to get an older sibling to stop another activity to play with them, to repair broken toys with tape or chewing gum, to manipulate a puzzle or plastic building blocks to get one uncooperative piece to fit, etc. The great 20th century mathematician and teacher George Polya stated that problem solving is "the most characteristically human activity." He pointed out that problem solving is a skill learned by doing, and that developing this skill requires a great deal of practice.

Games/Activities That Encourage the Use of Problem Solving Skills

One method that has been found to enhance children's reasoning skills is using adult-child conversations to play mental mathematics games. For example, once children are able to count beyond five, adults can give them basic oral story problems to solve (e.g., "If you have two plums and I give you two more, how many will you have?"). Using children's favorite foods in story problems, which takes advantage of their ready ability to envision these foods, is a good place to start. Thereafter, adults can add story problems involving pets, toys, cars, shopping, and other familiar objects/animals/activities. Experts advise adults not to restrict the types of problems presented to a child based solely on the child's grade level. Children can work with any situation if they can form mental imagery. Adults can sometimes insert harder tasks (e.g., problems involving larger numbers, problems involving division with remainders, or problems with negative number answers). Even toddlers can solve problems such as how to divide three cookies between two people. The division may not be fair, but it will likely be efficient. Adults should use the Socratic method, asking guiding questions to allow children to arrive at a solution to a problem themselves, rather than telling them a "right" answer.

Beneficial Practices of Playing Mental Math Games

Adults can use children's favorite foods and toys to pose story problems to children that involve addition and subtraction. For example, they can ask them questions like "If I give you [this many] more, how many will you have?" or "If we take away [this many], how many are left?" It is better to ask children questions than to give them answers. It is important to use turn taking. In this method, the adult poses a story problem to the child, and then the child gets to pose one to the adult. Adults must try to solve the problem, even if the child makes up numbers like "bazillion" or "eleventy." Games should be fun, not strictly factual like math tests. Adults can introduce age-appropriate story topics as children grow older. At the end of early childhood/around school age, children can handle the abstract algebraic concept of variables/unknown numbers (which some experts call "mystery numbers") and use this concept in games. Adults can pose riddles where "x" or "n" is the unknown number, and children must use an operation (e.g., $x + 4 = 7$) to solve the riddle.

Review Video: Addition and Subtraction
Visit mometrix.com/academy and enter code: 521157

Reasoning Skills

Communicating with Children to Promote Mathematical Reasoning Skills

Adults reciprocally talk to and listen to children during communication that is focused on using mathematical skills like problem solving, reasoning, making connections, etc. To promote young children's understanding, adults can express mathematical concepts using pictures, words, diagrams, and symbols. Encouraging children to talk with their peers and adults helps them clarify their own thoughts and think about what they are doing. Communicating with children about mathematical thinking problems also develops their vocabularies and promotes early literacy and reading skills. Adults should listen to what children want to say, and should have conversations with them. Communicating about math can also be accomplished through reading children's books that incorporate numbers and/or repetition or rhyme. In addition to talking, adults can communicate math concepts to children by drawing pictures or diagrams and using concrete objects (e.g., blocks, crayons, pieces of paper, fingers, etc.) to represent numbers and/or solve problems. Children also share their learning of math concepts through words, charts, drawings, tallies, etc. Even toddlers hold up fingers to tell others how old they are.

Using Reasoning Skills to Understand and Apply Early Mathematical and Scientific Concepts

A major component of problem solving is reasoning. Children reason when they think through questions and find usable answers. They use reasoning skills to make sense of mathematical and scientific subject matter. Children use several abilities during the reasoning process. For example, they use logic to classify objects or concepts into groups. They follow logical sequences to arrive at conclusions that make sense. They use their analytical abilities to explain their own thought processes. They apply what they have learned about relationships and patterns to help them find solutions to problems. They also use reasoning to justify their mental processes and problem solutions. To support children's reasoning, adults can ask children questions, give them time to think about their answers, and listen to their answers. This simple tactic helps children learn how to reason. Adults can also ask children why something is as it is—letting them think for themselves rather than looking for a particular answer—and listen to the ideas they produce.

Role of Representation Skills in Children's Learning

Young children develop an understanding of symbolic representation—the idea that objects, written letters, words, and other symbols are used to represent other objects or concepts—at an early age. This is evident in their make-believe/pretend play, and in their ability to learn written language and connect it to spoken language. As children develop early math skills, representing their ideas and information they acquire helps them organize, document, and share these ideas and facts with others. Children may count on their fingers; create tallies using check marks/tick marks and/or words; draw pictures or maps; and, as they grow older, make graphs. Teachers must help children apply mathematical process skills as they use learning center materials. For example, when a child enjoys sorting rocks by color, the teacher can state that the child is classifying them, bridging informal math activities with math vocabulary. Asking the child how s/he is categorizing the rocks emphasizes math vocabulary. Asking the child after s/he finishes what other ways s/he could classify the rocks encourages problem solving.

Making Connections and Helping Children Transition from Intuitive to Formal Math Thinking

Children informally learn intuitive mathematical thinking through their everyday life experiences. They naturally apply mathematical concepts and reasoning to solve problems they face in their environment. However, one frequent problem among children when they begin formal education is that they can come to see academic mathematics as a collection of procedures and rules, instead of viewing it as a means of finding solutions to everyday, real-life problems. This view will interfere with children's ability to apply the formal mathematics they learn to their lives in a practical and useful way. Teachers can help prevent this outcome by establishing the connection between children's natural intuitive math and formal mathematics. They can do this by teaching math through the use of manipulative materials familiar to children. They can use mathematics vocabulary words when describing children's activities, which enables children to develop an awareness of the natural mathematical operations they use in their daily lives. When a teacher introduces a new mathematical concept to children, s/he can give illustrative examples that draw upon the children's actual life experiences.

Relationship of Mathematics to Everyday Life and Other Academic Subjects

We use math throughout our lives during everyday activities. There are countless examples and combinations of various mathematical concepts in the real world. Additionally, math concepts inform other academic content areas, including music, art, and the sciences. Therefore, it is important for children not to view math as an isolated set of procedures and skills. Children comprehend math more easily when they can make connections, which involve applying common mathematical rules to multiple, varied functions, processes, and real-life activities. For example, adults can ask children to consider problems they encounter daily and solve them. When a parent asks a child to help put away groceries, the child practices sorting categories of foods and packages, and experiments with comparative package sizes and shapes. Parents need not be concerned with what specific mathematical processes are involved, but should simply look for examples of math in everyday life and expose children to these examples on a regular basis. For example, pouring liquid into containers of various sizes and speculating which one will hold the most is an easy, fun activity that incorporates a number of skills and concepts, including estimation, measurement, spatial sense, and conservation of liquid volume.

Patterns and Relationships

Patterns are generally defined as things that recur or are repeated regularly. Patterns can be found in images, sounds, numbers, events, actions, movements, etc. Relationships are generally defined as connections or associations between things that are identified and/or described using logic or reasoning. Being aware of patterns and relationships among aspects of the environment helps us comprehend the fundamental structure of these aspects. This awareness enables us to predict what will occur next in a series of events, even before it actually happens. This gives us more confidence in our environment and in our ability to interact with it. We find patterns and relationships in such areas of life as art, music, and clothing. Math-specific activities like counting numbers and working with geometrical shapes, lines, arcs, and curves also involve patterns and relationships. When children understand patterns and relationships, they can understand repetition; rhythm; categorization; and how to order things from smallest to biggest, from shortest to longest, etc.

Adults can help young children develop their understanding of patterns and relationships in life by looking at pictures and designs with them, encouraging and guiding them to identify patterns within drawings, paintings, and abstract designs such as prints on fabrics and other decorative designs. When children participate in movement activities, including dancing to music, running, skipping, hopping, playing simple musical instruments, etc., adults can help them identify patterns in their own and others' movements. Adults can encourage young children to participate in hands-on activities, such as stringing wood, plastic beads, or penne and other hollow dry pasta tubes onto pieces of string to make necklaces with simple patterns (e.g., blue-yellow-blue-yellow). As children grow older, adults can encourage them to create more complicated patterns. They can alternate a larger number of colors, and they can vary the numbers of each color in more complex ways (e.g., three blue, two yellow, one red, etc.).

Contribution of Number Sense and Number Operations to Math Comprehension

Counting is one of the earliest numeracy skills that young children develop. Even before they have learned the names of all the numbers, young children learn to count to three, then to five, etc. However, number sense involves a great deal more than just counting. Number sense includes understanding the various applications of numbers. For instance, we use numbers as tools for conveying and manipulating information, as tools for describing quantities, and as tools for characterizing relationships between or among things. Children who have developed number sense are able to count with accuracy and competence. Given a specific number, they can count upwards from that number. They can also count backwards. They are able to break down a number and then reassemble it. They are able to recognize relationships between or among different numbers. When children can count, are familiar with numbers, and have good number sense, they can also add and subtract numbers. Being familiar with numbers and being able to count easily helps young children understand all other areas of mathematics.

Activities to Help Develop Number Sense and Numeracy Skills

As children complete their daily activities, it is beneficial for adults to count real things with children and encourage them to count as well. This helps children understand numbers by using their own experiences with objects in the environment, and gives them practice counting and using numbers. To help children understand that we use numbers to describe quantities and relationships, adults can ask children to sort objects by size, shape, or color similarity. They can also ask children to sort objects according to their differences (e.g., which object is bigger/smaller). Adults can also discuss with children how numbers are used to find street addresses and apartment numbers, and to keep score during games. To help children count upwards and downwards with efficiency and accuracy, adults can point out that counting allows us to determine how many items are in a group. Adults should point to each object as they count it. They can count on their fingers and encourage young children to do the same. Adults should also help children count without repeating or skipping any numbers.

Spatial Sense and Geometry

Spatial sense is an individual's awareness of one's own body in space and in relation to the objects and other people around the individual. Spatial sense allows young children to navigate environmental spaces without colliding with objects and other people; to see and hear adequately, and to be aware of whether others can see and hear them; and to develop and observe a socially and culturally appropriate sense of their own and others' personal space. Geometry is the area of mathematics involving space, sizes, shapes, positions, movements, and directions. Geometry gives descriptions and classifications of our physical environment. By observing commonplace objects and spaces in their physical world, young children can learn about solid objects and substances, shapes, and angles. Adults can help young children learn geometry by identifying various shapes, angles, and three-dimensional figures for them; asking them to name these shapes, angles, and figures when they encounter them in the future; and asking them to describe different shapes, draw them in the air with their fingers, trace drawings of the shapes with their fingers, and then draw the shapes themselves.

Activities to Help Develop Spatial Sense and Geometry

Because it involves many physical properties like shape, line, and angle, as well as abstract concepts, young children learn geometry most effectively via hands-on activities. Learning experiences that allow them to touch and manipulate concrete objects, such as boxes, containers, puzzles, blocks, and shape sorters, usually work best. Everyday activities can also help children learn geometry concepts. For example, adults can cut children's sandwiches into various geometrical shapes and let children fit them together and/or rearrange them into new patterns. Children become better able to follow directions and navigate through space when they develop geometric knowledge and spatial sense. Adults can provide activities that promote the development of geometric knowledge and spatial sense. For example, they can let children get into and out of big appliance boxes; climb over furniture; and go into, on top of, out of, under, around, over, and through different objects and structures to allow children to experience the relationship between their bodies and space and solids. As they mature, children can play games in which they search for "hidden" shapes. Such shapes may be irregular, may lack flat bases, or may be turned in various directions.

Measurement

Measurement is the process of determining how long, wide, and tall something is physically and how much it weighs by using measuring units such as inches, feet, yards, square feet, ounces, and pounds. Measurement is also used to quantify time using units like seconds, minutes, hours, days, weeks, months, years, centuries, millennia, etc. Measurement is not just a formal means of quantifying size, area, and time. It is also an important method for young children to seek and identify relationships between and among things they encounter outside of school in everyday life.

When young children practice measuring things, they are able to understand not only the sizes of objects and beings, but also their comparative sizes (i.e. how large or small something is compared to another object used as a reference). Furthermore, they are able to figure out how big or little something is on their own.

While it is obviously important for children to eventually learn standardized measurement units like inches, feet, yards, etc., adults can facilitate early development of measurement skills by letting children choose their own measurement units. For example, they might use their favorite toy to describe a playmate or sibling as "three teddy bears tall"; or they might describe a room as "seven toy cars long." Similarly, when children are too young to know formal time measurements like minutes and hours, adults can support children's ability to quantify time using favorite TV shows. For example, four-year-olds can often relate to the idea of one episode of a show (whether it is 30 minutes or 60 minutes long) as a time measurement. Adults can apply this with statements like, "Daddy will be home in one episode." Numerous everyday activities, including grocery shopping, cooking, sewing, gardening, woodworking, and many others, involve measurement. Adults can ask children to help with these tasks, and then discuss measuring with children as they participate.

<u>Measurement of Time</u>
Younger children typically do not have an understanding of the abstract concept of time. However, adults can still help children understand that time elapses, and that we count/measure this process. For example, adults can ask younger children simple questions, such as "Who can stand on one foot longer?" This comparison strategy helps children figure out which of two or more actions/activities takes a longer/the longest period of time. Even when children do not yet understand what "five minutes" means, adults should still make such references (e.g., "You can play for five minutes longer, and then we must leave."). Repeating such references will eventually help children understand that time passes. Adults can time various everyday activities/events and tell children how long they took. They can also count the second hand's ticks on a watch/clock (e.g., "one second...two seconds...three seconds..."). This familiarizes children with counting, and with using counting to track the passage of time. Until children are old enough to understand abstractions like today/yesterday/tomorrow, adults can use concrete references like "after lunch" or "before bedtime."

Fractions

Fractions are parts or pieces of a whole. While adults understand this and do not remember ever not understanding it, very young children think differently in this regard. As Piaget showed, children in the preoperational stage of cognitive development cannot perform logical or mathematical mental operations. They focus on one property of an object rather than all of its properties, a practice he called centration. Hence, if you cut an apple into pieces, very young children see that there are more pieces than there were before, and they believe that several apple pieces are more than one apple. They cannot yet comprehend the logical sequence of dividing an apple into fractions. To comprehend fractions, children must know what a whole unit consists of, how many pieces the unit is divided into, and whether the pieces are of equal size. Adults can help children understand fractions through informal sharing activities, such as slicing up a pizza or a pan of brownies, and/or equally dividing household/preschool chores and play materials.

Estimation

Estimation is making an educated or informed guess about a measurement when no actual measurement is available. As adults, we often make estimates about the sizes of objects when we do not know their exact measurements, about the amounts of substances we have not actually measured, and about the numbers of small objects in large collections when we have not actually counted the objects. However, young children are in the process of learning the concepts of sizes and numbers. Children must comprehend concepts of comparison and relativity (e.g., larger, smaller, more, less, etc.) before they will be able to make accurate estimates. When children start to develop the ability to estimate amounts or sizes, this process helps them learn related math vocabulary words, such as "about" or "around," and "more than" and "less than" [something else]. Through estimating, they also learn how to make appropriate predictions and arrive at realistic answers. It is important for young children to learn how to make estimates, to recognize when it is appropriate to apply the estimation method, and to recognize when their estimates are reasonable.

Activities to Help Develop Estimation

To accustom young children to the idea of estimating, adults should regularly use words related to estimation in their conversations with children (e.g., "around," "about," "approximately," "near," "more than [some other amount or number]," "less than [some other amount or number]," "between [two numbers or amounts]," etc.). During everyday activities like shopping or eating, adults can ask children to estimate amounts of foods, numbers of items, or lengths of time. Later, adults can help children compare the actual outcome with their original estimate. This process helps children learn to make realistic/reasonable estimates. Activities promoting estimation skills can be very simple. Adults can ask children, for example, to guess which of their friends is tallest, and then test the accuracy of the guess using real measurements. When children grow older, adults can write down estimates and real measurements, and can then repeat the exercise described above or present a similar one. With repetition, children will eventually begin making more accurate estimates. The goal is not for children to come up with exact measurements, but ones that are close to actual amounts/numbers. Giving children opportunities to practice improves their estimating skills.

Probabilities and Statistics

In general, when people work with statistics, they present them in graphs or charts to organize them, interpret them, and make it easier to see relationships among individual statistics. Graphs are a visual alternative that depict mathematical information and show relationships among individual statistics, especially changes over time. Graphs also allow for the comparison of different groups. Probabilities indicate the likelihood that something will happen. Adults use probabilities to predict things, such as people's risks of developing or dying from various diseases or medical conditions; the chances of accidents; children's risks of experiencing academic difficulties, dropping out, or developing emotional and behavioral disorders; and the chances that a certain area will receive rain or snow. Scientists use probabilities to predict the likelihood of various behaviors or outcomes they are studying. They use statistics to show the numbers and proportions of responses or results obtained in research studies. Calendars are one type of chart. Adults can help children use them to organize daily and weekly activities, and to understand how we organize information.

Charts and Graphs

According to experts, almost every daily activity can be charted in some way. For example, adults can help children peel the little stickers off of plums, bananas, etc. and stick them to a piece of paper/poster board divided into columns. After a week, they can count each column to determine how many pieces of each kind of fruit they ate. Similarly, adults can show children how to use removable stickers or color forms to document the number of times they performed any daily activity. For example, children could place a color form near the telephone every time it rings and/or every time somebody picks it up to make a call. They could also place a color form near the front door every time somebody comes in, goes out, and/or rings the doorbell/knocks. This enables children to count the number of times given events occur by recording them. Some children are better able to understand math by viewing and making graphs. This is because creating graphs involves representing quantities visually instead of just listing numbers.

Counting

Counting is considered a math skill milestone for young children. Typical four-year-olds enjoy counting aloud. Experts identify three levels of counting. The first is counting from 1 to 12, which requires memorization. The second level is counting from 13 to 19, which requires not only memorization, but also an understanding of the more unusual rules for "teen" numbers. The third level is counting from 20 on. This process is very consistent, and the numbers are ordered according to regular rules. Experts in math education believe that at this level of counting, children are discovering a regular mathematical pattern for the first time, which is base ten (i.e. 20, 30, 40, 50, etc. are 2 tens, 3 tens, 4 tens, 5 tens, etc., and after the base a number between 1 and 9 is added). Researchers and educators in early childhood mathematics programs recommend encouraging children as young as four years old to learn to count up to 100. They find that doing this helps young children learn about and explore patterns in depth.

Perceiving and Identifying Shapes

The three levels of perceiving shapes that children typically move through sequentially are seeing, naming, and analyzing. Very young children recognize simple shapes like circles, squares, and triangles. As their cognitive and language skills develop, they learn the names for these shapes, and use these names to identify single shapes. The third level is analyzing each shape to understand its properties. Whereas identifying shapes visually is intuitive and based on association, analyzing their properties is more abstract, since a shape can have a number of different appearances. For example, three-year-olds can differentiate a triangle from other shapes. However, if you show them a very tall, skinny/short, wide/lopsided/crooked triangle, they will have trouble identifying it as a triangle. At the analysis level, children realize that a triangle has three sides, which are not necessarily equal in length. An activity that young children enjoy is closing their eyes, reaching into a bag of assorted shapes, finding a triangle by touch, and explaining why it is a triangle. This involves both the second and third levels of naming and analysis.

Integrating Math into Everyday Activities and Using Early Childhood Math Curricula

Integrating math into the context of everyday activities has been the philosophy of early childhood math education until recently. For example, when teachers have children line up, they ask them who is first, second, third, etc. to practice counting. When children play with blocks, teachers ask them to identify their shapes and whether one block is larger/smaller than another. During snack times, teachers help children learn 1:1 correspondence by having them place one snack on each plate. These activities are quite valuable. However, some educators maintain that they are insufficient when used on their own, because in larger classes it is not always possible to take advantage of "teachable moments" with every child. Therefore, this educational approach cannot be applied systematically. These educators recommend that in addition to integration strategies, EC teachers should use a curriculum. The HighScope curriculum, the Creative Curriculum, and Big Math for Little Kids are just a few examples. Many teachers combine several curricula, selecting parts of different programs. Using a curriculum allows teachers to use a more planned approach to integrate math into all activities.

Clinical Interview

Background, Method, and Advantages

Clinical interviews have long been used by individual and family therapists, as well as by researchers. Piaget used them along with observations and case histories to understand young children's thinking as he formulated his cognitive developmental theory. Interviewers ask structured/semi-structured/open-ended questions and listen to the responses, often recording them for accuracy. This method gives the interviewer a way to find out what the respondent is thinking and feeling inside, which cannot be determined by observing outward behaviors alone. In educational settings, a teacher might ask a child questions like, "How did you do this?" "What is happening now?" "Can you tell me more about this?" "Why are you doing this?" "What are you thinking about now?" etc. Flexible questioning helps uncover the child's thought process, which is what is leading him/her to engage in specific behaviors. Just observing the behaviors alone does not allow the child to express his/her knowledge. While fully interviewing each child in a classroom is not practical, teachers can adapt this method by asking clinical interview-type questions as part of their instruction.

Using Questioning

Teachers can gain a lot of information and insight about how children are learning math concepts by observing their behaviors. For children to actually express their knowledge and thinking processes, however, teachers must ask them questions. For example, when a teacher introduces new shapes to young children, s/he can ask them the shapes' names, how they differ from one another, and why they think the shapes differ. Teachers can then use children's various responses to elicit further responses from them. This technique requires children to use language in significant ways during math activities. Therefore, these activities not only teach math skills, but also promote literacy development. Asking clinical interview-type questions promotes children's development of math communication skills, one of the essential components of math education. Additionally, being able to put one's knowledge and thoughts into words is a skill that is very important in all areas of education, not just math education. Using clinical interview-type questions helps children learn to use language to explain their thinking, share ideas, and express themselves, promoting and strengthening children's awareness of the functions of mathematical language.

Characteristics of Young Children's Thinking and Learning That Inform EC Math Curricula

Young children think in concrete ways and cannot understand abstract concepts, so effective EC math curricula typically use many concrete objects that children can see, feel, and manipulate to help them understand math concepts. Young children also naturally learn through exploring their environments, so good EC math curricula have many exploration and discovery activities that allow and encourage hands-on learning. In everyday life, young children start to observe relationships as they explore their surroundings. They match like objects, sort unlike objects, categorize objects, and arrange objects in simple patterns based on shared or contrasting properties. They start to understand words and phrases like "a little," "a lot," "more," "less," and "the same [as…]." Preschoolers use available materials such as sticks, pieces of string, their feet, their hands, their fingers, etc. as tools to measure objects. They also use rulers, measuring cups, and other conventional tools. They use their measurements to develop descriptions, sequences, and arrangements, and to compare various objects.

Activities That Help Children Develop Spatial Awareness

When preschool children build structures with blocks and put together pieces of puzzles during play, they are not only having fun, but are also developing spatial awareness. The relationships of objects to each other and within space are important concepts for children to learn, and serve as a foundation for the principles of geometry and physics that children will learn later. When they are moving around, preschoolers begin to notice how other people and objects are positioned in space, and how their own bodies move through space in relationship to objects and other people. This type of spatial awareness supports children's developing gross motor skills, coordination, and social skills. Young children can and should learn a number of math concepts and skills, such as the ones recommended by preschool math curricula like the High Scope program's "Numbers Plus" preschool mathematics curriculum. These concepts and skills include number symbols and names, counting, shapes, spatial awareness, relationships of parts to the whole, measurement, units, patterns, and analyzing data.

Rational Numbers and Irrational Numbers

In mathematics, rational numbers are numbers that can be written as ratios or fractions. In other words, a rational number can be expressed as a fraction that has a whole number as the numerator (the number on top) and the denominator (the number on the bottom). Therefore, all whole numbers are automatically rational numbers, because all whole numbers can be written as fractions with a denominator of 1 (e.g., 5 = 5/1, 68 = 68/1, 237 = 237/1, etc.). Even very large, unwieldy fractions (e.g., 9,731,245/42,754,021) are rational numbers, because they can be written as fractions. Irrational numbers can be written as decimal numbers, but not as fractions, because the numbers to the right of the decimal point that are less than 1 continue indefinitely without repeating. For example, the value of pi (π) begins as 3.141592..., and continues without end. The square root of 2 ($\sqrt{2}$) = 1.414213.... There are an infinite number of irrational numbers between 0 and 1. However, irrational numbers are not used as commonly in everyday life as rational numbers.

Cardinal, Ordinal, Nominal, and Real Numbers

Cardinal numbers are numbers that indicate quantity. For example, when we say "seven buttons" or "three kittens," we are using cardinal numbers. Ordinal numbers are numbers that indicate the order of items within a group or a set. For example, when we say "first, second, third, fourth, fifth, etc.," we are using ordinal numbers. Nominal numbers are numbers that name things. For example, we use area code numbers along with telephone numbers to identify geographical calling areas, and we use zip code numbers to identify geographical mailing areas. Nominal numbers, therefore, identify categories or serve as labels for things. However, they are not related to the actual mathematical values of numbers, and do not indicate numerical quantities or operations. Real numbers include all rational and irrational numbers. Rational numbers can always be written as fractions that have both numerators and denominators that are whole numbers. Irrational numbers cannot, as they contain non-repeating decimal digits. Real numbers may or may not be cardinal numbers.

Activities and Games That Make Learning Fun

<u>Button Board</u>

By gluing buttons of various sizes and colors to a piece of cardboard, teachers can initiate a number of activities that help preschoolers learn math concepts while having fun. Preschoolers are commonly learning shapes and how to draw them. Teachers can give children lengths of string/twine/yarn or long shoelaces and show them how to wrap them around different buttons to form shapes like rectangles, triangles, and squares. To practice counting and 1:1 correspondence, teachers can ask children to wrap their string around a given number of buttons. Preschoolers need to learn the concept that spoken number words like "five" can equate to a group of five concrete objects (such as buttons), and this activity promotes that learning. The button board is also useful for giving preschool children practice with sorting or classifying objects into groups based on a common characteristic. For example, the teacher can ask children to wrap their pieces of string around all the big buttons, all the little buttons, only the red buttons, only the blue buttons, etc.

Beanbags and Hopscotch

Teachers can encourage preschool children's counting and number development by creating a grid on the floor with the numbers 1 to 10 using masking tape, construction paper, and markers. Teachers could also draw the grid outdoors by drawing on pavement with chalk. The teacher arranges the numbers in ascending order within the grid of 10 squares/rectangles. S/he asks the children if they can name these numbers. The teacher provides beanbags. Each child gets a chance to throw a beanbag into any one of the numbered squares. Children can see how far they can throw and/or practice their aim. Each child names the number inside the square/rectangle where his/her beanbag lands. The children then play a version of hopscotch by hopping from numbered square to square, collecting their beanbags, and then hopping back. If desired, the teacher can write the number each child's beanbag lands on onto a "scoreboard" graph. Children will observe his/her writing the same numbers found on the floor/ground onto a "scoreboard." Teachers can review learning after the game to assess whether children can count using number words, name selected numbers, and throw accurately with consistency.

Reusing Sectioned Plastic Trays

A teacher can wash and reuse the compartmentalized plastic trays from the grocery store that are used for vegetable and fruit to create a preschool counting activity. The teacher supplies beads, pennies, erasers, or other small objects, as well as about a dozen sticky notes. S/he writes a number on each note. For older preschoolers, the teacher can write the numeral and the word (e.g., "7" and "seven"). For younger children, the teacher can write the numeric symbol ("7," for example) plus seven dots or other marks as a clue to that number symbol. The teacher puts one numbered note in each compartment and the supply of small objects in the central dip compartment. Then, s/he guides each child to transfer the correct number of each small object to the correct compartment. The child should count aloud while transferring each small object, and should repeat this process until all compartments with a numbered sticky note have the correct number of objects. Children can then repeat the process to practice and perfect their counting, or the teacher can place notes with different numbers in the tray's compartments.

Fishing for Numbers

Teachers can help preschoolers practice identifying numbers and counting by creating a fun "fishing for numbers" game. Teachers cut 10 fish shapes that are about 6 inches long from pieces of construction paper that are different colors. Teachers then write a single number between 1 and 10 on each "fish." Near each fish "mouth," the teacher punches a hole and inserts a paper clip through it. The teacher makes "fishing rods" by tying strings to dowels and gluing a magnet to each string. After spreading out the fish so the children can easily see the numbers, the teacher assigns each child a number and they "fish" for it, picking up the fish by bringing the magnet close to the paper clip. The children then "reel in" their catches. This gives children practice correctly identifying number names. The game can be adapted for more advanced math concepts as well. For example, the teacher can cut out fish shapes of various sizes and have children "fish" for larger/smaller fish. The activity can also be adapted to promote literacy development. The teacher can write letters instead of numbers on the fish to give students practice with alphabet recognition, or s/he can write a Dolch word/sight word on each fish to give students practice recognizing and identifying important vocabulary words.

Collages

Fundamental math skills that prepare preschoolers for kindergarten include shape recognition. To introduce children to an activity they will view as fun rather than as work, teachers can show children how to make a collage of a familiar figure. This will also give children the opportunity to experiment with an artistic process. For example, they can create a Santa Claus or an Easter Bunny as a holiday art project. They can make collages of other imaginary/real people for various events/seasons/topics. Teachers cut out paper templates, including circles for heads, triangles for hats, squares for bodies, and narrow rectangular strips for limbs. First, they help children name each shape. They have each child trace the template shapes onto paper and cut them out with child-safe scissors. The teacher then instructs children to arrange their cutout shapes on a piece of cardboard/construction paper. Once they are in the correct positions, the children glue the shapes in place. Teachers can subsequently teach additional shapes (octagons, ovals, etc.), challenging children to make new, different collages.

Grab Bag

Young children learn to name numbers in a way that is similar to how they learn to recite alphabet letters. However, learning to associate number symbols with concrete objects in the real world environment is a major advance in their cognitive development. The concept of 1:1 correspondence entails matching number symbols to the quantities they represent, an essential early math skill. Teachers can support the development of this math skill with a simple "grab bag" game youngsters enjoy. The teacher writes a number from 1 to 10 on each of ten cards, folding each card in half and putting them into a paper lunch bag. The teacher provides each child with a handful of pennies/play coins/buttons/little blocks to use as counting tokens. Each child takes a turn closing his/her eyes and pulling a card out of the bag. The child reads the number on the card, counts out the corresponding number of pennies/tokens, and puts them with the card. As children learn, teachers can place additional and/or different numbers (e.g., 11 to 20) in the grab bag. To promote the development of early literacy skills, teachers can also include the name of the number on each card.

Pattern Resist Art

A significant mark of progress in early math skills development is the ability to not only identify various shapes, but also to draw them. Once young children develop this ability, they typically want to practice it all the time. Teachers can encourage this by helping children make pattern resist paintings. The teacher tapes white paper to children's tables/trays, gives them crayons, and invites them to fill the paper with drawings of different shapes of various sizes and colors. Teachers can introduce young children to new shapes (e.g., ovals, stars, crescent moons, etc.) by drawing them on separate pieces of paper for children to look at and copy. Then, the teacher replaces the crayons with water, watercolor paints, and brushes; shows the children how to dip brushes into paint and water to dilute the colors; and allows them to paint over their crayoned shapes, covering all the white paper with color. The children see the shapes show through the paint, creating the pattern resist. Dipping brushes and diluting various colors also develop children's color recognition skills and their hand-eye coordination.

Ice Cube Necklaces

In hot weather, making ice cube necklaces is a fun activity that helps young children cool off while learning to sequence objects. The activity also helps children develop their manual motor skills and learn about liquid and solid states of matter. Regular ice cube trays are fine; those with "fun-shaped" compartments are even better. The teacher cuts plastic drinking straws so that they will fit into each ice cube compartment. The children participate, watching and/or helping pour water into trays and adding various food colorings/fruit juices. The teacher places one straw clipping into each compartment. While putting the trays into the freezer, the teacher tells children that 32° Fahrenheit/0° Celsius is the temperature at which water freezes. Children practice making scientific observations by noting how long the water takes to freeze. They empty the cubes into a big bowl. The children put on bathing suits or other clothing that can get wet, and the class goes outdoors. The teacher provides strings that are knotted at one end, and calls out a color pattern (e.g., one blue cube, then a yellow cube, etc.). Children follow the teacher's instructions to create color-patterned necklaces they can tie, wear, and watch melt.

Red Rover

Red Rover is a good game for groups of children who are attending parties or playing outdoors at parks/playgrounds. Two teams take turns calling and roving. The child called runs to the other team and tries to fit into its line. If successful, s/he gets to call another player to bring back to his/her home team. If not, s/he joins the opposite team. The game continues until one team has no more members. Teachers can adapt this game to teach shape recognition by cutting out various shapes from construction paper of different colors and pinning a shape to each child's shirt. In large groups, more than one child can have the same shape or color. Instead of children's names, the teacher instructs players to use shapes and colors when calling (e.g., "Red Rover, Red Rover, blue circles come over!"). This supports the development of shape and color recognition skills. Teachers can vary action verbs (e.g., "....hop over/jump over/skip over") to support vocabulary development and comprehensive skills. When children perform such movements, they are also practicing and developing gross motor skills.

Counting on Fingers

A common practice among preschool children is counting on their fingers. Young children learn concretely before they develop abstract thought, so they must have concrete objects to work with to understand abstract mathematical concepts. They use their fingers to count because fingers are concrete. A simple activity that allows children to continue finger counting while removing additional visual support is "blind finger counting." Using eyesight to count objects we can see is relatively easy. However, when children cannot see objects, they must learn to count mentally instead. This allows them to take another step in their progress from concrete to abstract thinking. To count mentally without visual reinforcement takes practice. Teachers can tape a shoebox lid to the box and cut a small hole in it. Children can fit a hand through the hole, but cannot see inside. Children close their eyes; the teacher drops several small objects into the box; and each child reaches in, counting the objects using only touch. Varying objects and quantities maintains the fun of this activity.

Sorting and Categorization

One of the major learning accomplishments of young children is being able to identify similarities and differences among objects. Developing this ability enables children to sort like objects into groups, and to place objects into categories based on their differences. When preschoolers compare and contrast objects, they demonstrate an important early step in the development of critical thinking, analytical, and problem solving skills. For an easy, entertaining guessing game, adults can select assorted household items familiar to children and put them into a bag/pillowcase. They then give children various clues (e.g., "I stir lemonade with this...," "It's made of wood," "We keep it in the kitchen drawer...," etc.) and ask them to guess which items are in the bag. It is important to give young children one to two minutes to consider each clue before they make a guess. Adults repeat clues when children guess incorrectly. If children guess correctly, they are allowed to look inside the bag. Youngsters greatly enjoy seeing that the object they guessed is actually inside the bag. Adults can gradually make the game more challenging by beginning with very common objects, and then eventually progressing to more unusual ones.

Baking Cookies

Young children are typically curious about adult activities like baking. They usually want to know more about the process, and often ask many questions. They also love to be included and to participate, frequently offering/asking to help. Letting them help builds their self-esteem and self-efficacy (i.e. their confidence in their competence to accomplish a task). Adults can allow children to help while also providing instruction and practice with shape recognition, measurement, sorting, and categorization. The adult prepares a favorite cookie recipe. Some children can help measure ingredients, which helps develop the math skill of measurement. With the dough rolled out, children use cookie cutters of various shapes. Recognizing, naming, and selecting the shapes promote the development of shape recognition skills. Adults "shuffle"/mix the baked cookie shapes and have children separate cookies with like shapes into groups, which promotes sorting skills. Having children identify similar/different shapes, sizes, and colors promotes categorization skills. Arranging cookie shapes into patterns for children to identify promotes pattern recognition skills, which are necessary to the development of math skills and many other skills. Giving each child a cookie to eat afterward is naturally reinforcing.

Creative Crafts

Prerequisite abilities that young children need in order to develop early math skills include the ability to identify, copy, expand, and create patterns; as well as the ability to count. Adults can promote the development of these skills by giving children a craft project and introducing them to an interactive game they can play using their crafts. First, the children paint six ping pong balls red on one side to make red-and-white balls. Then, the children paint six ping pong balls blue on one side to make blue-and-white balls. Once the paint dries, the adult puts several balls into an egg carton so that one color is face up. The adult starts making a simple pattern (e.g., two white, then two red, then two blue), and asks each child to continue the pattern. Then, the adult allows each child to create his or her own original color patterns. Once a child masters creating patterns using solid colors, he or she can then use both the white and colored sides of the balls to create more complex patterns. Children can design an infinite number of patterns, which are often quite artistic.

Shape Matching Games

In one type of shape matching game, EC teachers help children make a game board out of construction paper that is shaped like a tree. Teachers first help the children cut a treetop and leaf shapes from green paper. They discuss children's preferences for tall/short and thick/thin trunks, giving them practice using descriptive vocabulary words, particularly ones related to size. This step builds both general and math concept vocabulary. Children cut trunks from brown paper and paste/glue them on the treetops. While out of the children's sight, the teacher cuts 5 to 10 (or more) pairs of shapes per child/tree from different colors of construction paper. Pairs should not match exactly (e.g., a blue square can be paired with a red square). The teacher glues one of each pair of shapes to each child's tree while the child is not looking. The teacher then gives each child the rest of the shapes, and invites children to see how quickly they can match each shape to its "partner" on the tree. The teacher can provide "warmer/cooler" distance clues, and should provide reinforcement each time a child correctly matches a pair of shapes. Teachers can make this activity more challenging by using more shapes and/or getting students to match shapes that are different sizes (e.g., children can be asked to match smaller diamonds to larger diamonds).

Homemade Beanbag Game

Young children enjoy tossing objects and practicing their aim. Adults can make a beanbag game that helps children learn numbers and identify sets, while also allowing them to construct their own game rules. First, the adult should cover five big, equally-sized coffee (or similar) cans with paper that is adhesive on one side. The adult should then use markers to write a number from 1 to 5 and draw the corresponding number of dots on each can. The next step is to fill 15 tube socks with beans and knot/tie/sew them shut. The following numerals and the corresponding number of dots should be written on each homemade beanbag using markers: the number 1 on five beanbags, the number 2 on four beanbags, the number 3 on three beanbags, the number 4 on two beanbags, and the number 5 on one beanbag. Next, the adult should attach the cans to the floor with tape or Velcro. Then, the adult should mark a line on the floor that children must stand behind, and should direct children ONLY to toss the beanbags into the cans. Children will devise various games/rules. First, they may simply toss the beanbags into the cans; then, some may try to toss beanbags into a can that has the same number as the one marked on the beanbag. Eventually, some may throw three beanbags into the "3" can. They may/may not keep score. Allowing children to determine the details and rules gives them an opportunity to develop their imagination and decision making skills, and to create their own games while learning number and set identification.

<u>Guessing Game</u>

Adults can adapt the format of "20 Questions," "I Spy," and other similar guessing games to focus on numbers and help children learn number concepts. For example, adults could say, "I'm thinking of a number from 1 to 10…." and then give children 10 guesses. Adults give children cues as they guess, such as "higher" and "lower," to help them narrow down the number of possible correct answers. As children improve, adults can increase the number range (e.g., from 0 to 50) or use larger numbers (e.g., from 20 to 40). As children's skills and self-confidence develop, adults can reverse roles, having children think of numbers and give clues while adults guess. Young children enjoy the fun of guessing, getting closer using clues, deducing correct answers, and fooling adults with their own clues. Concurrently, they learn to describe numbers, compare them, and sequence them. Adults can make the game more difficult by limiting the number of guesses allowed and/or setting time limits. They can make it easier by providing a written number line for children to reference. This game requires no materials (or just a basic number line), is a great way to pass time, and entertains children while helping to develop numeracy skills.

<u>Arts and Crafts</u>

According to the U.S. Department of Agriculture, preschoolers need three ½-cup servings of fruit and three ½-cup servings of vegetables daily. However, many young children are picky/resistant. Adults can motivate them to eat produce with a "food rainbow" project. Adults show children a picture of a rainbow, and discuss its colors and their sequence (teaching some earth science, optics, and color theory!). A fun art project is allowing students to color their own rainbows, which improves fine motor skills. Then, adults can have children cut out pictures from grocery circulars and name each food. The adult can help children find one healthy fruit/vegetable for each color, gluing each food to its corresponding stripe on the rainbow. Adults can then help children pull apart cotton balls and glue them to their rainbow pictures to represent clouds. Children can then post their food rainbows on refrigerators as artwork and as healthy eating reminders. At the bottom, children can draw and color one box (bottom-up) for each food they eat (e.g., blue = blueberries, orange = carrots, red = apples, etc.) to create a bar graph. Children should try to "eat" the entire rainbow every week. This activity gives children the opportunity to produce colorful art, eat better, track and document their diets, and develop graphing skills.

Review Video: <u>Bar Graph</u>
Visit mometrix.com/academy and enter code: 226729

Treasure Hunt

A treasure hunt is an ideal outdoor activity for young children, and can also be adapted for indoor fun. The treasure can be anything (e.g., a small toy/play money/chocolate "coins"/rocks spray painted gold or silver, etc.). The adult should put the treasure in a paper bag marked with a large X. The adult should hide it somewhere where it is not visible, but will not be overly difficult for children to find. Then, the adult should make a treasure map, using few words and many pictures, sketching landmark objects in the area (trees, houses, etc. if the activity will be done outdoors, and furniture, walls, etc. if the activity will be done indoors). The adult should ensure the map is developmentally appropriate for young children, and that they will be able to read it independently. Adults with time and motivation can make the map look authentic by soaking it in tea/coffee, drying it in a 200° oven, or even charring its edges. Adults should include a dotted line on the map that reinforces the simple directions and indicates the path to the treasure, which is indicated on the map by a large X. Children have fun, use their imaginations, make connections between symbols and images to corresponding real-world physical objects, and begin learning to read maps.

Pasta Necklace

Stringing beads/noodles is an activity that helps young children develop hand-eye coordination, which they will need for writing and other everyday activities that require fine motor coordination. Noodles are typically the perfect size for young children's hands. They are inexpensive, usually costing less than comparably-sized beads. Moreover, pasta is non-toxic, an advantage when working with little persons who put things in their mouths. Hollow, tubular noodles like penne, ziti, wagon wheels, etc. are ideal. Fishing line/craft beading string/other stiff string is best; soft, limp string/yarn is harder for young children to manipulate. Using multicolored vegetable pasta removes the need to use markers or dye to add color. If using white pasta, children can color the noodles with markers, but adults should keep in mind that the ink can bleed onto skin/clothes even when it is dry. Adults should cut pieces of string that are long enough to allow children to easily slip the necklaces on and off after they are tied. Adults should also use a knot to secure a noodle to one end of the string. By providing more than one noodle shape, adults can invite children to string the noodles to create patterns, which develops pattern recognition and pattern creation abilities. These abilities also inform repetition, rhythm, categorization, and sequencing skills, which are important in math, music, art, literature, clothing design, etc.

Number Dash

A game for young children that some educators call "Number Dash" (Miller, ed. Charner, 2009) builds foundational math concepts and skills, while providing physical activity. It can involve small or large groups (the referenced authors say "the more the merrier"). Help children write large numbers on a paved area with sidewalk chalk. Make sure numbers are spread far enough apart so children will not collide while running. There should be one of each number for each child (e.g., six "1s," "2s," "3s," etc. if there are six children). Use chalk colors that contrast with the pavement color to ensure the numbers will be highly visible. Tell children to run ("dash") to whichever number you call out and stand on it until you call another number. Call out numbers randomly. Encourage children who have located the number to help their classmates/playmates. This game develops gross motor skills, number writing skills, and number recognition skills. It also provides experience with playing organized games, following rules, following directions, and cooperating with and helping others. This game can also be played with letters, colors, and/or shapes.

Introducing Standard Measurement Using a Ruler

A teacher is introducing standard measures to her class as part of a unit on measurement, one of the early math skills. She shows the children a ruler, explaining that it is one foot long, and that we can use it to measure inches and parts of inches. She demonstrates placing the ruler on paper to measure a given length, explaining that the ruler can also be used as a straight edge for drawing lines. One child asks, "How come you started with zero? Why don't you start with one like when we count?" The teacher responds, "That's a very good question! Zero means none/nothing. When we count, we start with one because we already have at least one of something. When you were born, you were not one year old; your age began at zero. After a year, on your first birthday, you were one year old. We also begin measuring distances at zero/none/nothing. The first piece/unit of measurement is one, not two. The distance from zero to one is equal to one. To get to one inch, for example, we need to start at zero."

Learning About Geometric Shapes and Their Properties

A teacher has been working with students to help them develop their shape identification skills. They can recognize shapes by sight, and have also learned the defining properties of different shapes (number of sides, etc.). The teacher shows the class this figure:

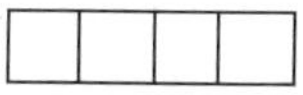

She asks how many rectangles they can find in the figure. One student answers, "There is one rectangle," which is incorrect because a square is a rectangle; this figure has four rectangles that are squares. Moreover, the entire figure is itself a rectangle. Another student therefore says, "There are five rectangles." This response is also incorrect. Two adjacent squares also form a rectangle; this means there are three additional rectangles. Three adjacent squares also form a rectangle; this means there are two additional rectangles. Thus, the figure has a total of 10 rectangles. Solving this puzzle requires the use of many skills, including analyzing visual information, synthesizing visual information, recognizing patterns, recognizing shapes, and identifying the properties of shapes.

Collecting, Organizing, and Displaying Data Using Sticky Notes and a Teacher-Made Chart

A preschool teacher is teaching her group of ten children about basic data collection, data arrangement, and data display. She shows children yellow, blue, and green sticky notes, and has each child select his/her favorite color. Five children choose yellow notes, three select blue, and two choose green. By choosing one of three colors, each child has participated in data collection. The teacher draws lines to divide a sheet of paper into three columns, and labels each column with one of the colors. She helps the children place their chosen sticky notes in the correct columns. By arranging the colored sticky notes into columns, the teacher and children have organized the data they gathered. Once all notes are in their proper color columns, the completed chart is an example of how collected, organized data can be displayed.

	Yellow sticky note	
	Yellow sticky note	
Blue sticky note	Yellow sticky note	
Blue sticky note	Yellow sticky note	Green sticky note
Blue sticky note	Yellow sticky note	Green sticky note
BLUE	**YELLOW**	**GREEN**

Selecting One of Three Colors of Sticky Notes, Organizing Them by Color, and Displaying Them

The teacher had ten children each choose one of three colors of sticky notes, an example of basic data collection. She used a chart with three columns to organize the children's choices as follows:

	Yellow sticky note	
	Yellow sticky note	
Blue sticky note	Yellow sticky note	
Blue sticky note	Yellow sticky note	Green sticky note
Blue sticky note	Yellow sticky note	Green sticky note
BLUE	**YELLOW**	**GREEN**

The chart displays the collected and organized data. The teacher asks the children which color was chosen the most. Seeing five yellow notes, they answer, "yellow." She asks which color was chosen the least, and they say, "green." She asks them to use numbers to arrange the color choices from most popular to least popular. They arrive at, "five yellow, three blue, and two green." Together, the teacher and the children point to and count ten children. She tells them five equals half of ten, and asks which color half of the children chose. Together, they figure out it was yellow. These are examples of analyzing and interpreting data.

Science Concepts Young Children Learn During Everyday Activities

Science entails asking questions, conducting investigations, collecting data, and seeking answers to the questions asked by analyzing the data collected. Natural events that can be examined over time and student-centered inquiry through hands-on activities that require the application of problem solving skills are most appropriate for helping young children learn basic science. In their everyday lives, young children develop concepts of 1:1 correspondence through activities like fitting pegs into matching holes or distributing one item to each child in a class. They also develop counting concepts by counting enough items for each child in the group or counting pennies in a piggy bank. They develop classification concepts when they sort objects into separate piles according to their shapes or some other type of category (e.g., toy cars vs. toy trucks). When children transfer water, sand, rice, or other substances from one container to another, they develop measurement concepts. As they progress, children will apply these early concepts to more abstract scientific ideas during grade school.

Science Concepts Infants and Toddlers Learn in Normal Developmental Processes

Infants use their senses to explore the environment, and are motivated by innate curiosity. As they develop mobility, children gain more freedom, allowing them to make independent discoveries and think for themselves. Children learn size concepts by comparing the sizes of objects/persons in the environment to their own size, and by observing that some objects are too large to hold, while others are small enough to hold. They learn about weight when trying to lift various objects. They learn about shape when they see that some objects roll away, while others do not. Babies learn temporal sequences when they wake up wet and hungry, cry, and have parents change and feed them. They also learn this concept by playing, getting tired, and going to sleep. As soon as they look and move around, infants learn about space, including large/small spaces. Eventually, they develop spatial sense through experiences like being put in a playpen/crib in the middle of a large room.

Toddlers naturally sort objects into groups according to their sizes/shapes/colors/uses. They experiment with transferring water/sand among containers of various sizes. They learn part-to-whole relationships by building block structures and then dismantling them.

Naturalistic, Informal, and Structured Learning Experiences

Children actively construct their knowledge of the environment through exploring it. Young children's learning experiences can be naturalistic (i.e. spontaneously initiated by the child during everyday activities). During naturalistic learning, the child controls his/her choices and actions. Informal learning experiences also allow the child to choose his or her actions and activities, but they include adult intervention at some point during the child's engagement in naturalistic pursuits. In structured learning experiences, the adult chooses the activities and supplies some direction as to how the child should perform the associated actions. One consideration related to EC learning that teachers should keep in mind is that within any class or group of children, there are individual differences in learning styles. Additionally, children from different cultural groups have varying learning styles and approaches. EC teachers can introduce science content in developmentally appropriate ways by keeping these variations in mind.

Naturalistic Learning Experiences

Motivated by novelty and curiosity, young children spontaneously initiate naturalistic experiences during their everyday activities. Infants and toddlers in Piaget's sensorimotor stage learn by exploring the environment through their senses, so adults should provide them with many objects and substances they can see, hear, touch, smell, and taste. Through manipulating and observing concrete objects/substances, preschoolers in Piaget's preoperational stage begin learning concepts that will enable them to perform mental operations later on. Adults should observe children's actions and progress, and should give positive reinforcement in the form of looks, facial expressions, gestures, and/or words encouraging and praising the child's actions. Young children need adult feedback to learn when they are performing the appropriate actions. For example, a toddler/preschooler selects a tool from the toolbox, saying, "This is big!" and the mother responds, "Yes!" A four-year-old sorting toys of various colors into separate containers is another example of a naturalistic experience. A five-year-old who observes while painting that mixing two colors yields a third color is yet another example.

Informal Learning Experience

Informal learning experiences involve two main components. First, the child spontaneously initiates naturalistic learning experiences during everyday activities to explore and learn about the environment. Second, the adult takes advantage of opportunities during naturalistic experiences to insert informal learning experiences. Adults do not plan these in advance, but take advantage of opportunities that occur naturally. One way this happens is when a child is on the right track to solve a problem, but needs some encouragement or a hint from the adult. Another way is when the adult spots a "teachable moment" during the child's naturalistic activity, and uses it to reinforce a basic concept. For example, a three-year-old might hold up three fingers, declaring, "I'm six years old." The parent says, "Let's count fingers: one, two, three. You're three years old." Or, a teacher asks a child who has a box of treats if s/he has enough for the whole class, and the child answers, "I don't know." The teacher then responds, "Let's count them together," and helps the child count.

Structured Learning Experiences

Naturalistic learning experiences are spontaneously initiated and controlled by children. Informal learning experiences involve unplanned interventions by adults during children's naturalistic experiences, which is when adults offer suitable correction/assistance/support. Structured learning experiences differ in that the adult pre-plans and initiates the activity/lesson, and provides the child with some direction. For example, a teacher who observes a four-year-old's need to practice counting can give the child a pile of toys, and then ask him/her how many there are. To develop size concepts, a teacher can give a small group of children several toys of different sizes, and then ask the children to inspect them and talk about their characteristics. The teacher holds up one toy, instructing children to find one that is bigger/smaller. If a child needs to learn shape concepts, the teacher might introduce a game involving shapes, giving the child instructions on how to play the game. Or, a first grade teacher, recognizing the importance of the concept of classification to the ability to organize scientific information, might ask students to bring in bones to classify during a unit on skeletons.

Kindergarten Activity for Collecting and Organizing Data

Preschoolers and kindergarteners continue their earlier practices of exploration to learn new things, and they apply fundamental science concepts to collect and organize data in order to answer questions. To collect data, children must have observation, counting, recording, and organization skills. One activity kindergarteners and teachers enjoy is growing bean sprouts. For example, the teacher can show children two methods: one using glass jars and paper towels saturated with water, the other using cups of dirt. The children add water daily as needed, observe developments, and report to the teacher, who records their observations on a chart. The teacher gives each child a chart that they add information to each day. The children count how many days their beans took to sprout in the glass jars and in the cups of dirt. They then compare their own results for the two methods, and they compare their results to those of their classmates. The children apply concepts of counting, numbers, time, 1:1 correspondence, and comparison of numbers. They also witness the planting and growing process.

Science Process Skills

Science process skills include observation (using the senses to identify properties of objects/situations), classification (grouping objects/situations according to their common properties), measurement (quantifying physical properties), communication (using observations, classifications, and measurements to report experimental results to others), inference (finding patterns and meaning in experiment results), and prediction (using experimental experience to formulate new hypotheses). Inferences and predictions must be differentiated from objective observations. Classification, measurement, and comparison are basic math concepts which, when applied to science problems, are called process skills. The other science process skills named, as well as defining and controlling variables, are equally necessary to solve both science and math problems. For example, using ramps can help young children learn basic physics concepts. Teachers ask children what would happen if two balls were rolled down a ramp at the same time, if two balls were rolled down a ramp of a different height/length, if two ramps of different heights/lengths were used, etc. In this activity, children apply the scientific concepts of observation, communication, inference, and prediction, as well as the concepts of height, length, counting, speed, distance, and comparison.

Scientific Method

Children are born curious, and naturally engage in problem solving to learn. Problem solving and inquiry are natural child behaviors. EC teachers can use these behaviors to promote children's scientific inquiry. Scientific inquiry employs the scientific method. The first step in the method is to ask a question, which is another natural child behavior. Just as adult scientists formulate research questions, the first step of the scientific method for children is asking questions they want to answer. Next, to address a question, both adults and children must form a hypothesis (i.e. an educated guess about what the answer will be). The hypothesis informs and directs the next steps: designing and conducting an experiment to test whether the hypothesis is true or false. With teacher instruction/help, children experiment. For example, they might drop objects of different weights from a height to see when each lands, as Galileo did. Teachers help record outcomes. The next steps are deciding whether the results prove/disprove the hypothesis and reporting the results and conclusions to others.

Review Video: The Scientific Method
Visit mometrix.com/academy and enter code: 191386

Physical Science and Matter

Physical science is the study/science of the physical universe surrounding us. Everything in the universe consists of matter (i.e. anything that has mass and takes up space) or energy (i.e. anything that does not have mass or occupy space, but affects matter and space). Three states of matter are solid, liquid, and gas. Solids preserve their shape even when they are not in a container. Solids have specific, three-dimensional/crystalline atomic structures and specific melting points. Liquids have no independent shape outside of containers, but have specific volumes. Liquid molecules are less cohesive than solid molecules, but more cohesive than gas molecules. Liquids have flow, viscosity (flow resistance), and buoyancy. Liquids can undergo diffusion, osmosis, evaporation, condensation, solution, freezing, and heat conduction and convection. Liquids and gases are both fluids, and share some of the same properties. Gases have no shape, expanding and spreading indefinitely outside of containers. Gases can become liquid/solid through cooling/compression/both. Liquids/solids can become gaseous through heating. Vapor is the gaseous form of a substance that is solid/liquid at lower temperatures. For example, when water is heated it becomes steam, a vapor.

Review Video: States of Matter
Visit mometrix.com/academy and enter code: 742449

Liquids

Of the three states of matter—solid, liquid, and gas—liquids have properties that fall somewhere in between those of solids and gases. The molecules of solids are the most cohesive (i.e. they have the greatest mutual attraction). Gas molecules are the least cohesive, and liquid molecules are in between. Liquids have no definite shape, while solids do. Liquids have a definite volume, whereas gases do not. The cohesion of liquid molecules draws them together, and the molecules below the surface pull surface molecules down, creating surface tension. This property can be observed in containers of water. Liquid molecules are also attracted to other substance's molecules (i.e. adhesion). Surface tension and adhesion combined cause liquids to rise in narrow containers, a property known as capillarity. Liquids are buoyant (i.e. they exert upward force so objects which have more buoyancy than weight float in liquids, while objects which have more weight than buoyancy sink in liquids). Liquids can be made solid by freezing, and can be made gaseous by heating/evaporation. Liquids can diffuse, which means they can mix with other molecules. Liquid diffusion across semi-permeable membranes is known as osmosis.

Solids

Solids are one of the three forms of matter. The other two are liquids and gases. Solids maintain their shape when they are not inside of containers, whereas liquids and gases acquire the shapes of containers holding them. Containers also prevent liquids and gases from dispersing. Of the three forms of matter, solids have the most cohesive molecules. Solid molecules are most attracted to each other, and solid molecules are held together most strongly. Solid atoms are organized into defined, three-dimensional, lattice-shaped patterns (i.e. they are crystalline in structure). Solids also have specific temperatures at which they melt. Some substances that seem solid, such as plastic, gel, tar, and glass, are actually not true solids. They are amorphous solids because their atoms do not have a crystalline structure, but are amorphous (i.e. the positions of their atoms have no long-range organization). They also have a range of melting temperatures rather than specific melting points.

Review Video: Amorphous Solids
Visit mometrix.com/academy and enter code: 121001

Review Video: Balance of Forces That Make a Solid
Visit mometrix.com/academy and enter code: 519967

Gases

Gas, liquid, and solid are the three states of matter. Gases have the least cohesive (i.e. mutually attracted) molecules of the three states of matter, while solids have the most cohesive molecules. Gases do not maintain a defined shape, while solids do. If not contained within a receptacle, gases spread and expand indefinitely. Gases can be elementary or compound. An elementary gas is composed of only one kind of chemical element. At normal temperatures and pressures, 12 elementary gases are known: argon*, chlorine, fluorine, helium*, hydrogen, krypton*, neon*, nitrogen, oxygen, ozone, radon*, and xenon*. Compound gases have molecules containing atoms of more than one kind of chemical element. Carbon monoxide (which contains one carbon and one oxygen atom) and ammonia (which contains nitrogen and hydrogen atoms) are common compound gases. Heating gas molecules/atoms charges them electrically, making them ions. Plasma combines positive gas ions and electrons. Some gases are colorless and odorless, while others are not. Some burn with oxygen, while others do not. *Noble/inert gases have single atoms that do not normally form compounds with other elements.

Light

Reflection and Scattering

When a beam of light hits a smooth surface like a mirror, it bounces back off that surface. This rebounding is reflection. In physics, the law of reflection states that "the angle of incidence equals the angle of reflection." This means that when light is reflected, it always bounces off the surface at the same angle at which it hit that surface. When a beam of light hits a rough rather than a smooth surface, though, it is reflected back at many different angles, not just the angle at which it struck the surface. This reflection at multiple and various angles is scattering. Many objects we commonly use every day have rough surfaces. For example, paper may look smooth to the naked eye, but actually has a rough surface. This property can be observed by viewing paper through a microscope. Because light waves striking paper are reflected in every direction by its rough surface, scattering enables us to read words printed on paper from any viewing angle.

Absorption

When light strikes a medium, the light wave's frequency is equal or close to the frequency at which the electrons in the medium's atoms can vibrate. These electrons receive the light's energy, making them vibrate. When a medium's atoms hang on tightly to their electrons, the electrons transmit their vibrations to the nucleus of each atom. This makes the atoms move faster and collide with the medium's other atoms. The energy the atoms got from the vibrations is then released as heat. This process is known as absorption of light. Materials that absorb light, such as wood and metal, are opaque. Some materials absorb certain light frequencies but transmit others. For example, glass transmits visible light (and therefore appears transparent to the naked eye), but absorbs ultraviolet frequencies. The sky looks blue because the atmosphere absorbs all colors in the spectrum except blue, which it reflects. Only blue wavelengths/frequencies bounce back to our eyes. This is an example of subtractive color, which we see in paints/dyes and all colored objects/materials. Pigments absorb some frequencies and reflect others.

Refraction

When light moves from one transparent medium to another (e.g., between water and air/vice versa), the light's speed changes, bending the light wave. It bends either away from or toward the normal line, an imaginary straight line running at right angles to the medium's surface. We easily observe this bending when looking at a straw in a glass of water. The straw appears to break/bend at the waterline. The angle of refraction is the amount that the light wave bends. It is determined by how much the medium slows down the light's speed, which is the medium's refraction index. For example, diamonds are much denser and harder than water, and thus have a higher refraction index. They slow down and trap light more than water does. Consequently, diamonds sparkle more than water. Lenses, such as those in eyeglasses and telescopes, rely on the principle of refraction. Curved lenses disperse or concentrate light waves, refracting light as it both enters and exits, thus changing the light's direction. This is how lenses correct (eyeglasses) and enhance (telescopes) our vision.

Magnetism

Magnetism is the property some objects/substances have of attracting other materials. The form of magnetism most familiar to us is certain materials attracting iron. Magnets also attract steel, cobalt, and other materials. Generators supplying power include magnets, as do all electric motors. Loudspeakers and telephones contain magnets. Tape recorders use magnets. The tape they play is magnetized. Magnets are used in compasses to determine the location of north and various corresponding directions. In fact, the planet Earth is itself a giant magnet (which is why compasses point north). Hence, like the Earth, all magnets have two poles: a north/north-seeking pole and a south/south-seeking pole. Opposite poles attract, and like poles repel each other. Magnets do not need to touch to attract/repel each other. A magnet's effective area/range is its magnetic field. All materials have some response to magnetic fields. Magnets make nearby magnetic materials into magnets, a process known as magnetic induction. Materials that line up parallel to magnetic force field lines are paramagnetic, while materials that line up perpendicular to magnetic force field lines are diamagnetic.

Modern Theory of Magnetism and What Scientists Do/Do Not Know

Scientists have known about the effects of magnetism for hundreds of years. However, they do not know exactly what magnetism is, or what causes it. French physicist Pierre Weiss proposed a theory of magnetism in the early 20th century that is widely accepted. This theory posits that every magnetic material has groups of molecules—domains—that function as magnets. Until a material is magnetized, its domains have a random arrangement, so one domain's magnetism is cancelled out by another's. When the material comes into a magnetic field—the range/area wherein a magnet is effective—its domains align themselves parallel to the magnetic field's lines of force. As a result, all of their north-seeking/north poles point in the same direction. Removing the magnetic field causes like poles to repel one another as they normally do. In easily magnetized materials, domains revert to random order. In materials that are harder to magnetize, domains lack sufficient force to disassemble, leaving the material magnetized. Later versions of Weiss's theory attribute domain magnetism to spinning electrons.

Review Video: Magnets
Visit mometrix.com/academy and enter code: 570803

Insulation, Conduction, and the Flow of Electricity

The smallest units of all matter are atoms. The nuclei of atoms are orbited by negatively charged electrons. Some materials have electrons that are strongly bound to their atoms. These include air, glass, wood, cotton, plastic, and ceramic. Since their atoms rarely release electrons, these materials have little or no ability to conduct electricity, and are known as electrical insulators. Insulators resist/block conduction. Metals and other conductive materials have free electrons that can detach from the atoms and move around. Without the tight binding of insulators, materials with loose electrons enable electric current to flow easily through them. Such materials are called electrical conductors. The movements of their electrons transmit electrical energy. Electricity requires something to make it flow (i.e. a generator). A generator creates a steady flow of electrons by moving a magnet close to a wire, creating a magnetic field to propel electrons. Electricity also requires a conductor (i.e. a medium through which it can move from one place to another).

Movement of Electrical Currents by a Generator

Magnetism and electricity are related, and they interact with each other. Generators work by using magnets near conductive wires to produce moving streams of electrons. The agent of movement can range from a hand crank, to a steam engine, to the nuclear fission process. However, all agents of movements operate according to the same principle. A simple analogy is that a generator magnetically pushes electrical current the way a pump pushes water. Just as water pumps apply specific amounts of pressure to specific numbers of water molecules, generator magnets apply specific amounts of "pressure" to specific numbers of electrons. The number of moving electrons in an electrical circuit equals the current, or amperage. The unit of measurement for amperage is the ampere, or amp. The amount of force moving the electrons is the voltage. Its unit of measurement is the volt. One amp equals 6.24×10^{18} electrons passing through a wire each second. For example, a generator could produce 1 amp using 6 volts when rotating 1,000 times per minute. Today's power stations rely on generators.

Positions and Motions of Objects and Newton's Laws of Physics

Moving physical objects changes their positions. According to Newton's first law of motion, an object at rest tends to stay at rest and an object in motion tends to stay in motion, unless/until an opposing force changes the object's state of rest/motion. For example, an object at rest could be a small rock sitting on the ground. If you kick the rock into the air, it moves through the air. The rock will continue to move, but when a force like gravity acts on it, it falls/stops moving. The resulting motion from kicking the rock illustrates Newton's third law of motion: for every action there is an equal and opposite reaction. The acceleration or increase in velocity (a) of an object depends on its mass (m) and the amount of force (F) that is applied to the object. Newton's second law of motion states that $F = ma$ (force equals mass times acceleration). Thus, moving objects maintain their speeds unless some force(s) cause acceleration or slowing/stopping, as frictional forces do.

Heat

Heat is transmitted through conduction, radiation, and convection. Heat is transmitted in solids through conduction. When two objects at different temperatures touch each other, the hotter object's molecules are moving faster. They collide with the colder object's molecules, which are moving slower. As a result of the collision, the molecules that are moving more rapidly supply energy to the molecules that are moving more slowly. This speeds up the movement of the (previously) slower moving molecules, which heats up the colder object. This process of transferring heat through contact is called thermal conductivity. An example of thermal conductivity is the heat sink. Heat sinks are used in many devices. Today, they are commonly used in computers. A heat sink transfers the heat building up in the computer processor, moving it away before it can damage the processor. Computers contain fans, which blow air across their heat sinks and expel the heated air out of the computers.

Acoustical Principles and the Human Hearing Process

When any physical object moves back and forth rapidly, this is known as vibration. The movements that occur during vibration disturb the surrounding medium, which may be solid, liquid, or gaseous. The most common sound conducting medium in our environment is gaseous: our atmosphere (i.e. the air). An object's vibratory movements represent a form of energy. As this acoustic energy moves through the air, it takes the form of waves, sound waves specifically. The outer ear receives and amplifies the sound and transmits it to the middle ear, where tiny bones vibrate in response to the sound energy and transmit it to the inner ear. The inner ear converts the acoustic energy into electrical energy. The electrical impulses are then carried by nerves to the brain. Structures in the brain associated with hearing receive these electrical signals and interpret them (i.e. make sense of them) as sounds. The ears' reception of sound waves is auditory sensation, and the brain's interpretation of them is auditory perception.

Solar System

Solar System's Location and Components

The universe is composed of an unknown (possibly infinite) number of galaxies or star systems, such as the Spiral Nebula, the Crab Nebula, and the Milky Way. Our sun, Sol, is one of billions of stars in the Milky Way. The solar system's planets are held in position at varying distances (according to their size and mass) from the Sun by its gravitational force. These planets orbit or revolve around the Sun. From the closest to the Sun to the farthest away, the solar system's planets are Mercury, Venus, Earth, Mars, Jupiter, Saturn, Uranus, and Neptune. Pluto was historically included as the ninth planet, but was demoted to a "dwarf planet" by the International Astronomical Union in 2006. Due to angular momentum, planets rotate on their axes, which are imaginary central lines between their north and south poles. One complete Earth rotation equals what we perceive as one 24-hour day. As the Earth turns, different portions face the Sun. These receive daylight, while the portions turned away from the Sun are in darkness. One complete revolution of the Earth around the Sun represents one calendar year.

Pluto

Since more powerful observatories have enabled greater detection and measurement of celestial objects, the International Astronomical Union has defined three criteria for defining a planet. First, it must orbit the Sun. Pluto meets this criterion. Second, it must have enough gravitational force to shape itself into a sphere. Pluto also meets this criterion. Third, a planet must have "cleared the neighborhood" in its orbit. This expression refers to the fact that as planets form, they become the strongest gravitational bodies within their orbits. Therefore, when close to smaller bodies, planets either consume these smaller bodies or repel them because of their greater gravity, clearing their orbital area/"neighborhood." To do this, a planet's mass must sufficiently exceed the mass of other bodies in its orbit. Pluto does not meet this criterion, having only 0.07 times the mass of other objects within its orbit. Thus, astronomers reclassified Pluto as a "dwarf planet" in 2006 based on its lesser mass and the many other objects in its orbit with comparable masses and sizes.

Earth

Earth is roughly spherical in shape. Its North and South Poles at the top and bottom are farthest away from and least exposed to the Sun, so they are always coldest. This accounts for the existence of the polar ice caps. The Equator, an imaginary line running around Earth at its middle exactly halfway between the North and South Poles, is at 0° latitude. Sunrises and sunsets at the Equator are the world's fastest. Days and nights are of virtually equal length at the Equator, and there is less seasonal variation than in other parts of the world. The equatorial climate is a tropical rainforest. Locations close to the North Pole, like Norway, are at such high latitudes that their nights are not dark in summertime, hence the expression "Land of the Midnight Sun." They also have very little light in wintertime. As Earth revolves around the Sun over the course of a year, the distance and angle of various locations relative to the Sun change, so different areas receive varying amounts of heat and light. This is what accounts for the changing seasons.

Rocks Found on the Earth's Surface

Sedimentary Rocks

Earth's rock types are sedimentary, igneous, and metamorphic. These categories are based on the respective processes that form each type of rock. Igneous rocks are formed from volcanoes. Metamorphic rocks are formed when igneous and sedimentary rocks deep inside the Earth's crust are subjected to intense heat and/or pressure. Sedimentary rocks are formed on Earth's surface, and characteristically accumulate in layers. Erosion and other natural processes deposit these layers. Some sedimentary rocks are held together by electrical attraction. Others are cemented together by chemicals and minerals that existed during their formation. Still others are not held together at all, but are loose and crumbly. There are three subcategories of sedimentary rock. Clastic sedimentary rocks are made of little rock bits—clasts—that are compacted and cemented together. Chemical sedimentary rocks are frequently formed through repeated flooding and subsequent evaporation. The evaporation of water leaves a layer of minerals that were dissolved in the water. Limestone and deposits of salt and gypsum are examples. Organic sedimentary rocks are formed from organic matter, such as the calcium left behind from animal bones and shells.

Metamorphic Rocks

Sedimentary rocks are formed on the Earth's surface by layers of eroded material from mountains that were deposited by water, minerals like lime, salt and gypsum deposited by evaporated floodwater, and organic material like calcium from animal bones and shells. Igneous rocks are formed from liquid volcanic rock—either magma underground or lava on the surface—that cools and hardens. Metamorphic rocks are formed from sedimentary and igneous rocks. This happens when sedimentary and/or igneous rocks are deep inside the Earth's crust, where they are subjected to great pressure or heat. The process of metamorphism does not melt these rocks into liquid, which would happen inside a volcano. Rather, the pressure and/or heat change the rocks' molecular structure. Metamorphic rocks are thus more compact and denser than the sedimentary or igneous rocks from which they were formed. They also contain new minerals produced either by the reconfiguration of existing minerals' structures or by chemical reactions with liquids infiltrating the rock. Two examples of metamorphic rocks are marble and gneiss.

Igneous Rocks

Igneous or volcanic rocks are formed from the magma emitted when a volcano erupts. Magma under the Earth's surface is subject to heat and pressure, keeping it in liquid form. During a volcanic eruption, some magma reaches the surface, emerging as lava. Lava cools rapidly in the outside air, becoming a solid with small crystals. Some magma does not reach Earth's surface, but is trapped underground within pockets in other rocks. Magma cools more slowly underground than lava does on the surface. This slower cooling forms rocks with larger crystals and coarser grains. The chemical composition and individual cooling temperatures of magma produce different kinds of igneous rocks. Lava that cools rapidly on the Earth's surface can become obsidian, a smooth, shiny black glass without crystals. It can also become another type of extrusive rock, such as andesite, basalt, pumice, rhyolite, scoria, or tuff (formed from volcanic ash and cinders). Magma that cools slowly in underground pockets can become granite, which has a coarse texture and large, visible mineral grains. It can also become another type of intrusive rock, such as diorite, gabbro, pegmatite, or peridotite.

Erosion

Erosion is a natural process whereby Earth's landforms are broken down through weathering. Rain, wind, etc. wear away solid matter. Over time, rain reduces mountains to hills. Rocks break off from mountains, and in turn disintegrate into sand. Weathering and the resulting erosion always occur in downhill directions. Rain washes rocks off mountains and down streams. Rains, rivers, and streams wash soils away, and ocean waves break down adjacent cliffs. Rocks, dirt, and sand change their form and location through erosion. They do not simply vanish. These transformations and movements are called mass wasting, which occurs chemically (as when rock is dissolved by chemicals in water) or mechanically (as when rock is broken into pieces). Because materials travel as a result of mass wasting, erosion can both break down some areas and build up others. For example, a river runs through and erodes a mountain, carrying the resulting sediment downstream. This sediment gradually builds up, creating wetlands at the river's mouth. A good example of this process is Louisiana's swamps, which were created by sediment transported by the Mississippi River.

Living Organisms

All living organisms have fundamental needs that must be met. For example, plants that grow on land need light, air, water, and nutrients in amounts that vary according to the individual plant. Undersea plants may need less/no light. They need gases present in the water, but not in the air above the water. Like land plants, they require nutrients. Like plants, animals (including humans) need air, water, and nutrients. They do not depend on light for photosynthesis like most plants, but some animals require more light than others, while others need less than others or none at all. Organisms cannot survive in environments that do not meet their basic needs. However, many organisms have evolved to adapt to various environments. For example, cacti are desert plants that thrive with only tiny amounts of water, and camels are desert animals that can also go for long periods of time with little water. Penguins and polar bears have adapted to very cold climates. Internal cues (e.g., hunger) and external cues (e.g., environmental change) motivate and shape the behaviors of individual organisms.

Types of Animal Life Cycles

Most animals, including mammals, birds, fish, reptiles, and spiders, have simple life cycles. They are born live or hatch from eggs, and then grow to adulthood. Animals with simple life cycles include humans. Amphibians like frogs and newts have an additional stage involving a metamorphosis, or transformation. After birth, they breathe through gills and live underwater during youth (e.g., tadpoles). By adulthood, they breathe through lungs and move to land. Butterflies are examples of animals (insects) that undergo complete metamorphosis, meaning they change their overall form. After hatching from an embryo/egg, the juvenile form, or larva, resembles a worm and completes the majority of feeding required. In the next stage, the pupa does not feed, and is typically camouflaged in what is called an inactive stage. Mosquito pupae are called tumblers. The butterfly pupa is called a chrysalis, and is protected by a cocoon. In the final stage, the adult (imago) grows wings (typically) and breeds. Some insects like dragonflies, cockroaches, and grasshoppers undergo an incomplete metamorphosis. There are egg, larva, and adult stages, but no pupa stage.

Ecology

Ecology is defined as the study of interactions between organisms and their environments. Abiotic factors are the parts of any ecosystem that are not alive, but which affect that ecosystem's living members. Abiotic factors also determine the locations of particular ecosystems that have certain characteristics. Abiotic factors include the sunlight; the atmosphere, including oxygen, hydrogen, and nitrogen; the water; the soil; the temperatures within a system; and the nutrient cycles of chemical elements and compounds that pass among living organisms and their physical environments. Biotic factors are the living organisms within any ecosystem, which include not only humans and animals, but also plants, microorganisms, etc. The definition of biotic factors also includes the interactions that occur between and among various organisms within an ecosystem. Sunlight determines plant growth and, hence, biome locations. Sunlight, in turn, is affected by water depth. Ocean depths where sunlight penetrates, called photic zones, are where the majority of the photosynthesis on Earth occurs.

Review Video: Photosynthesis
Visit mometrix.com/academy and enter code: 227035

Organism Reproduction

A few examples of the many ways in which organisms reproduce include binary fission, whereby the cells of prokaryotic bacteria reproduce; budding, which is how yeast cells reproduce; and asexual reproduction. The latter occurs in plants when they are grafted, when cuttings are taken from them and then rooted, or when they put out runners. Plants also reproduce sexually, as do humans and most other animals. Animals, including humans, produce gametes (i.e. sperm or eggs) in their gonads through the process of meiosis. Gametes are haploid, containing half the number of chromosomes found in the body's cells. During fertilization, the gametes combine to form a zygote, which is diploid. It has the full number of chromosomes (half from each gamete), which are arranged in a genetically unique combination. Zygotes undergo mitosis, reproducing their gene combination with identical DNA sequences in all new cells, which then migrate and differentiate into organizations of specialized organs and tissues. These specialized organs in biologically mature organisms, alerted by signals such as hormonal cues, undergo meiosis to create new haploid gametes, beginning the cycle again.

Plant Reproduction

Most plants can reproduce asexually. For example, cuttings can be rooted in water and planted. Some plants put out runners that root new growths. Many plants can be grafted to produce new ones. Plants also reproduce sexually. Plants' sexual life cycles are more complex than animals', since plants alternate between haploid form (i.e. having a single set of chromosomes) and diploid form (i.e. having two sets of chromosome) during their life cycles. Plants produce haploid cells called gametes* (equivalent to sperm and egg in animals) that combine during fertilization, producing zygotes (diploid cells with chromosomes from both gametes). Cells reproduce exact copies through mitosis (asexual reproduction), becoming differentiated/specialized to form organs. Mature diploid plants called sporophytes—the plant form we usually see—produce spores. In sporophytes' specialized organs, cells undergo meiosis. This is part of the process of sexual reproduction, during which cells with half the normal number of chromosomes are produced before fertilization occurs. The spores produced by the sporophyte generation undergo mitosis, growing into a haploid plant of the gametophyte generation that produces gametes*. The cycle then repeats.

Ecological Relationships

Organisms interact, both with other organisms and their environments. Relationships wherein two differing organisms regularly interact so that one or both of them benefit are known as ecological relationships. In mutualistic relationships, both organisms benefit. For example, bacteria live in termites' digestive systems. Termites eat wood. However, they cannot digest the cellulose (the main part of plant cell walls) in wood. The bacteria in termites' guts break down the cellulose for them, releasing the wood's nutrients. Reciprocally, the termites as hosts give the bacteria a home and food. In commensalistic relationships, one organism benefits and the other one is unaffected. One example is barnacles attaching to whales. Barnacles, which are filter feeders, benefit from the whales' swimming, which creates currents in the water that bring the barnacles food. The whales are not disturbed by the barnacles. In parasitic relationships, the parasite benefits, but the host suffers. For example, tapeworms inside animals' digestive tracts get nutrients. The hosts lose the nutrients stolen by the worms, and can sustain tissue damage because of the presence of the tapeworms.

Levels of Self-Awareness

Even newborns demonstrate differentiation of body through rooting and orienting responses, which are triggered by touching the cheek. (1) <u>Differentiation</u>: At this level, children recognize correspondence between their movements and those in the mirror, and differentiate their mirror images from other individuals. They differentiate the self. (2) <u>Situation</u>: At this level, beyond matching the surface properties of what they feel and what they see in the mirror, and beyond differentiating the self, children realize that their reflection is unique to their self. They also realize that their body/self and other things are situated in space. (3) <u>Identification</u>: At this level, beyond differentiating and situating the self, children now identify their reflection as "me." When psychologists place a dot/sticky note on a child's face before s/he looks in a mirror, the child reaches toward his or her own face to touch/remove it, demonstrating self-recognition and an emerging self-concept. (4) <u>Permanence</u>: At this level, children identify a permanent self across time and space, recognizing themselves in photos and home movies regardless of year/age/clothing/location/setting, etc. (5) <u>Self-consciousness/"meta" self-awareness</u>: At this level, children recognize their self from others' perceptions/perspectives as well as their own. They experience pride, shame, and other "self-conscious" feelings.

Progression of Self-Awareness Between Birth and Two Years of Age

From birth, infants differentiate their bodies from the environment, and differentiate internal from external stimuli (i.e. self-touch/stimulation vs. non-self/others' touch/stimulation). From two months old, babies show a sense of their body's position relative to other things in their environment. They systematically imitate others' facial expressions and movements. They also explore and consider the environment's responses to their own actions. Additionally, they smile and socially interact face-to-face with others, showing a new sense of shared experiences. By four months, infants systematically reach for and touch objects they see, showing hand-eye coordination. From four to six months, they regulate their reaching based on their sitting/posture and balance. By six months, babies can differentiate video of themselves from that of other, identically dressed babies. Babies between the ages of four and seven months can differentiate live video of themselves from that of experimenters imitating the same behaviors. By two years, children develop an understanding of symbolic representation, and know that mirror images and pictures of themselves stand for themselves. They also start to develop language skills and develop the ability to engage in pretend play.

Factors Contributing to the Development of Interpersonal Relationships

(1) The first basic factor that contributes to the development of interpersonal relationships in early childhood is child-adult relationships. These are the earliest interpersonal interactions, and start to develop at birth. When children's needs are consistently met by adults, children learn to trust adults. In his famous theory of development, Erikson called the first stage of psychosocial development and the central conflict of infancy basic trust vs. mistrust. (2) The second factor is autonomy, which refers to making decisions and doing things for oneself. Toddlers develop autonomy. Erikson called his second stage of psychosocial development and the central conflict of toddlerhood autonomy vs. shame and self-doubt. Children who are consistently given developmentally appropriate autonomy are more likely to respect others' autonomy, a key feature of interpersonal development. (3) The third basic factor is pretend play, which emerges as children's understanding of symbolic representation develops and they begin to use things to stand for other things. Pretending to be grown-ups engaging in adult activities helps children learn about adult skills and roles. Interacting with peers in make-believe scenarios prepares children for real-life adult interactions. Constructive ECE approaches do not involve punishing children who have not developed sufficient interpersonal relationship awareness. Instead, they encourage adults to teach children socially acceptable behaviors and reward positive interpersonal interactions.

Interactions and Relationships with Peers

By the time they are a year old, most babies have begun to interact with their peers, particularly when it comes to activities involving concrete objects. The development of walking and talking abilities in normally developing toddlers by the time they are two years old enables them to coordinate their behavior when playing with peers. They can imitate one another's behaviors, and can alternate roles during play, as they understand symbolic representation and can create make-believe scenarios. Pretend play increases from the ages of three to five years, as do prosocial behaviors, which include helping and caring for others. At the same time, egocentrism and aggressive behaviors decrease, as children are more able to consider others' viewpoints and feelings. Emergent social interaction skills such as these form the foundation for children's early peer relationships. When children demonstrate preferences for certain peers and choose to play and otherwise interact with them over others, this is the beginning of what will develop into preschool friendships, which are based mostly upon mutual play activities and exchanges of concrete things. Children tend to form daycare friendships with members of their own sex only over time.

Current Views on Conflict Resolution

ECE experts find that while many elementary and secondary schools have implemented conflict resolution programs, children should start learning how to resolve conflicts at younger ages. For example, experts associated with the successful HighScope EC curriculum have designed an approach to conflict resolution for children from 18 months to six years old. The steps in EC conflict resolution are similar to those used to resolve adult conflicts in education, law, labor relations, and diplomacy. Such problem solving steps have also been found to be effective in daycares, Head Start programs, preschools, nursery schools, and kindergartens. While the steps are the same regardless of the age of the children, they are applied differently according to children's developmental levels. Adults supply much of the language to describe problems and solutions for toddlers; preschoolers can often do this themselves. After experiencing the conflict resolution process, elementary school students can frequently function as mediators for classmates. Even very young children with limited language skills should be encouraged to agree and participate through nodding, pointing, and answering yes/no questions. Conflict mediation and resolution skills help children develop lifelong problem solving and social skills.

Conflict Resolution Approach Designed for Children Between the Ages of 18 Months and 6 Years

The steps used to mediate EC conflicts resemble the steps used in adult mediation. For example, EC experts at the HighScope Educational Research Foundation designed a conflict resolution approach for children aged 18 months to 6 years that consists of these six steps: (1) Calmly approach the children who are in conflict and stop any harmful behaviors. (2) Acknowledge what the children are feeling. (3) Collect information about the conflict. (4) Restate what the problem is. (5) Ask children to suggest possible solutions, and help them choose one together. (6) Follow up by providing support as needed. Experts find that children as young as 18 months demonstrate emergent problem solving skills. They observed young children's abilities to immediately and honestly express emotions. They noted that with adult support, children can frequently generate simple and creative problem solutions. While school conflict resolution is typically aimed at preventing violence, teaching conflict resolution skills can also help children develop the social skills needed to grow into independent, productive members of society.

Parenting Styles Identified by Psychologists

Psychologists (Baumrind, 1967; Maccoby & Martin, 1983) have identified four parenting styles: (1) Authoritarian These parents are strict, punitive, demanding, and unresponsive. They do not explain reasons for their rules to children. Their children are obedient and proficient at completing academic/technical tasks, but they are less competent socially and less happy. They also have lower self-esteem. (2) Authoritative This is the ideal parenting style. These parents are responsive, nurturing, and forgiving. They are assertive without being restrictive or intrusive. They set rules, but explain them. They are democratic, address children's questions and input, and use supportive rather than punitive discipline. Their children tend to be competent, successful, and happy. (3) Permissive These parents are indulgent, lenient, nontraditional, and undemanding. They are nurturing, responsive, and communicative with children, but do not expect their children to show much maturity and/or self-control. They avoid confrontation and seldom use discipline, often acting more like friends than parents. Their children's self-regulation skills are deficient and they are not as happy as many of their peers. They tend to have difficulty with authority and perform poorly in school. (4) Uninvolved These parents are undemanding, unresponsive, and uncommunicative. They meet their children's basic needs, but are relatively detached from their children's lives. In extreme cases, these parents may neglect/reject children. Their children have low self-esteem and lack self-control.

Family Systems Theory

Characteristics of Families Affecting the Early Development of Children

Family systems theory studies the behavior of the family unit rather than the behavior of individual family members. Family behavior includes the interactions among family members and how the family unit responds to stress. Some family characteristics have been identified as particularly pertinent to ECE (Christian/NAEYC, 2006). They are boundaries, roles, rules, hierarchy, climate, and equilibrium. Hierarchy is a family's balance of power, control, and decision making. Culture, religion, age, gender, and economic status influence the family hierarchy, which shifts whenever changes occur in the family's composition. Climate refers to a family's emotional quality, and includes the physical and emotional environments in which families raise children. These environments reflect a family's belief about families and children. Family climate determines whether a child feels safe/loved/supported or frightened/rejected/unhappy in his/her family. Equilibrium refers to the family's balance and consistency. It is disrupted by stress and change, and is maintained or protected by family traditions, customs, and rituals.

Family Influences on Early Childhood Development

Family systems theory examines not individual behavior but family behavior, including communication, interaction, connection/separation, loyalty/autonomy, and responses to stress within the context of the family unit. Family system components particularly influential in early childhood development include the following: (1) Boundaries This refers to limits, separateness, and togetherness (i.e. what/whom the family includes/excludes). "Disengaged" families value independence over belonging, and are open to new input. "Enmeshed" families value togetherness over autonomy, and have more closed/restrictive boundaries. (2) Roles Each family member has a role (e.g., helper, clown, peacemaker, victim, rescuer, etc.). Family members also tend to assume these roles in social, school, and work contexts. (3) Rules Family interaction rules have long-term influences (e.g., parents who view life as predictable are likely to plan ahead, while those who view life as less controllable may not prevent/avoid problems, but rather address them as they occur). Family rules can be unspoken. Also, the rules of family cultures and school cultures can conflict. The other three of the six prominent influences on EC are hierarchy, climate, and equilibrium.

Human Socialization and Major Socializing Agencies

Socialization is the process by which individuals learn their society's norms, values, beliefs, and attitudes; and what behaviors society expects of them relative to those parameters. This learning is imparted by agencies of socialization. The family, peer groups, and leaders of opinion are considered primary socializing agencies. The family is probably the most important because it has the most significant influence on individual development. Families influence the self-concept, feelings, attitudes, and behaviors of each individual member. As children grow, they encounter peer groups throughout life, which also establish norms and values to which individual group members conform. Schools, workplaces, religions, and mass media are considered secondary socializing agencies. Schools dictate additional academic and behavioral norms, values, beliefs, and behaviors. Workplaces have their own cultures that continue, modify, and/or add to the values and behaviors expected of their members. Religions also regulate members' behavior through beliefs, values, goals, and norms that reflect moral principles within a society. Mass media communicate societal conventions (e.g., fashion/style), which enables individuals to learn and adopt new behaviors and/or lifestyles.

Influence of Institutions on the Development of Individual Identity, Relationships, Beliefs, and Behaviors

Family is the first and most important socializing agent. Infants learn behavioral patterns from mothers. Their primary socialization is enabled through such early behaviors as nursing, smiling, and toddling. Babies soon interact with other family members. All the infant's physiological and psychological needs are met within the family. Babies learn their sleeping, eating, and toileting habits within the family environment. Babies' personalities also develop based on their early experiences, especially the amounts and types of parental love and affection they receive. School is also a critical socializing agent. Children extend family relationships to society when they go to school. Cognitive and social school experiences develop children's knowledge, skills, beliefs, interests, attitudes, and customs, and help determine the roles children will play when they become adults. In addition to family relationships, receiving reinforcements at school and observing and imitating teachers influence personality development. Peer groups that are based on friendships, shared ideas, and common interests in music, sports, etc. teach children/teens about conforming to rules and being rejected for not complying with these rules. Mass media like TV profoundly influence children, both negatively and positively.

Culture

While no single definition of culture is universally embraced, one from the cultural anthropology perspective is "...a system of shared beliefs, values, customs, behaviors and artifacts that members of society use to cope with their worlds and with one another, and that are transmitted from generation to generation through learning." (Bates and Fratkin, 2002) Cultural groups are based on a wide range of factors, including geographic location, occupation, religion, sexual orientation, income, etc. Individuals may follow the beliefs and values of more than one culture concurrently. For instance, recent immigrants often espouse values and beliefs from both their original and adopted countries. Traditionally, social systems like education and healthcare have approached cultural diversity by focusing on race/ethnicity and common beliefs about various racial/ethnic group customs. These are frequently generalizations (e.g., lumping Mexican, Cuban, and Puerto Rican cultures together and describing them as "Latino" culture). This type of practice can lead to oversimplified stereotypes, and therefore to unrealistic behavioral expectations. Service professionals need more detailed knowledge of cultural complexities and subtleties to effectively engage and interact with families.

Collectivism and Individualism

Certain world cultures are oriented more toward collectivism, while others are oriented more toward individualism. Native American, Latin American, Asian, and African cultures are more often collectivistic, focusing on interdependence, social interactions, relationships, and connections among individuals. North American, Canadian, European, and Australian cultures are more commonly individualistic, focusing on independence, uniqueness, self-determination, and self-actualization (realizing one's full potential). Individualism favors competition and distinguishing oneself as an individual, while collectivism favors cooperation that promotes and contributes to the harmony and well-being of the group. Individualist cultures value teaching young children object manipulation and scientific thinking, while collectivist cultures value social and relational behaviors. For example, adults in collectivist cultures may interpret a child's first steps as walking toward the adult, while adults in individualist cultures interpret them as developing motor skills and autonomy. These interpretations signify what each culture values most, forming the child's cultural orientation early in life. The planning and design of educational and other programs should be informed by a knowledge of these and other cultural differences.

Cultural Competence

Culturally Competent Professionals

A culturally competent professional demonstrates the ability to enable "...mutually rewarding interactions and meaningful relationships in the delivery of effective services for children and family whose cultural heritage differs from his or her own." (Shonkoff, National Research Council and Institute of Medicine, 2000) Providing interpreters and/or translators does not on its own constitute cultural competence. Hiring racially diverse educational staff in schools is also not enough. Culturally competent educators demonstrate highly developed self-awareness of their own cultural values and beliefs. They must also have and/or develop communication skills that allow them to elicit information from students and families regarding their own cultural beliefs. Further, they must be able to understand how diverse cultural views may affect a child's education, as well as how parents/families receive, comprehend, interpret, and respond to educators' communications. Therefore, educators must develop communication skills to meet educational goals.

Aspects of Cultural Competence

It is important for educational professionals to acquire and demonstrate cultural competence at the individual level to effectively interact with individual children and their families. Moreover, cultural competence is also important at the program level, the school level, and the system level. According to the National Center for Cultural Competence (NCCC), system level cultural competence is a continuing process that includes "...valuing diversity, conducting self-assessments (including organizational assessments), managing the dynamics of differences, acquiring and institutionalizing cultural knowledge, and adapting to the diversity and cultural contexts of the individuals and communities served." (Goode, 2001) Individual educational interactions are informed by a knowledge of cultural diversity and of the importance of such diversity in educational settings, an ability to adapt to the population's cultural needs, and a willingness to engage in ongoing self-reflection. This same set of knowledge and skills is also applied at the system level. Family engagement is important in EC care and education. This includes understanding the developmental needs of families as well as their children, especially when families and/or children speak different languages.

Acculturation Versus Assimilation

Acculturation describes the process whereby people adapt or change their cultural traditions, values, and beliefs as a result of coming into contact with and being influenced by other cultures over time. Some cultures adopt certain characteristics from other cultures they are exposed to, and two or more separate cultures may sometimes virtually fuse. However, assimilation, wherein various ethnic groups unite to form a new culture, is different from acculturation. One dominant culture may assimilate others. A historical example is the Roman Empire, which forced many members of ancient Greek, Hebrew, and other cultures to abandon their own cultures and adopt Roman law, military allegiance, traditions, language, religion, practices, and customs (including dress). The extent of a diverse cultural group's acculturation influences how it interacts with social systems like education and healthcare. Groups that are strongly motivated to maintain their cultural identity may interact less with mainstream systems that significantly conflict with or vary from their own cultural beliefs.

Measuring the Acculturation of Immigrants and Diverse Cultural Groups in America

Social scientists currently use indices such as people's country of birth, how long they have lived in America, their knowledge of the English language, and their level of English language use to study acculturation. However, these factors are measured not because they are the core elements of acculturation, but because they are easier to validly and reliably measure than the underlying cultural beliefs, attitudes, and behaviors they reflect, which are harder to quantify. The interactions between American educators and culturally diverse families can be problematic on both sides. Educators have difficulty interacting, communicating, and collaborating with families that come from a variety of other countries, speak various other languages, and differ in their degree of acculturation to American culture. On the other hand, immigrant and culturally diverse families encounter a foreign language, different cultural customs and practices, and an unfamiliar educational system with different methods of assessment, placement, curriculum planning and design, instruction, and evaluation—not to mention different special education laws and procedures. Thus, the acculturation challenges related to interactions between American educators and culturally diverse families are bilateral.

Cultural Differences in Parents' Goals for Raising Their Children

Depending on their cultural group, parents have varying goals for their children, and use different practices to achieve those goals. For example, research on four different cultural groups in Hawaii found the following differences related to what parents visualized when they pictured their children as successful adults: Native Hawaiians most wanted their children to have social connections, be happy in their social networks, and demonstrate self-reliance as adults. Caucasian American parents most valued self-reliance, happiness, spontaneity, and creativity as developmental outcomes for their children. Filipino American parents most valued the development of traits related to obedience, citizenship, respect for authority, and good conduct and manners in their children. Japanese American parents placed priority on their children's achievement, as well as their ability to live well-organized lives, stay in contact with family, and master the demands of life. Such distinct, significant differences imply that these parent groups would vary in how they would respond to young children's assertive behaviors, in their disciplinary styles (e.g., permissive, authoritative, authoritarian), and in the emphasis they would place on activities focusing on physical and cognitive skill mastery vs. social competence and connection.

<u>Educational Services Accessed by Different Cultures</u>

Parents in America have been found to show distinct preferences for the kinds of care and educational services they access for their children. For example, Caucasian parents in America are more likely to turn to preschool centers for help with their young children's care and instruction. This preference is influenced not only by custom, but also by scientific evidence that center-based preschool experience improves children's skills and prepares them for school. Hispanic parents in America are more likely to use home-based and/or family-based care settings. This preference probably reflects the more collectivist Hispanic perspective, which places more importance on social relationships than on structured learning in early childhood. Educators can take a culturally competent approach to such cultural diversity by looking for ways in which young children's school readiness skills can be promoted in family and home-based child care settings.

<u>Different Views on Care, Education, and the Nature of Their Cognitive Abilities</u>

Depending on their native culture, parents vary in terms of the early experiences they select for their young children. For example, Latino parents tend to prefer family-based/home-based care. White parents tend to prefer center-based daycare and education designed to promote school readiness. Another cultural difference is parental beliefs about children's learning capacities. For example, research in California found that the majority of Latino parents believed their children's learning capacity is set at birth; only a small minority of white parents held this belief. Parents subscribing to a transactional child development model view the complex interaction between child and environment as creating a dynamic developmental process. These parents are more likely to value the stimulation of early childhood development, seek/implement activities that will provide such stimulation, and access early intervention services for children with developmental delays/difficulties. Parents subscribing to a view of fixed, innate cognitive capacity are less likely to believe their children's cognitive abilities can be influenced by educational experiences, and may not see the benefits of or seek out early learning stimulation and intervention.

Cultural and Other Influences and How Much Parents in America Read to Their Children

Researchers analyzing national early childhood surveys have identified significant variations in how often white, Asian, and Hispanic parents read to their young children. This variation is not solely due to varying cultural values. Additional factors include parents' financial limitations; time limitations; familiarity and comfort with accessing libraries and other government resources, websites, etc.; and literacy levels in both English and their native languages. Educators must realize that trying to encourage or even teach parents to read to their children earlier and/or more often is unlikely to be successful if parents do not place value or priority on the benefits of being read to, or do not view the outcomes of reading aloud to children as benefits. Reading to children is known to promote school readiness and academic success. Educators should also understand that some children, despite not being read to in early childhood, become successful adults. Additionally, some cultures, including African Americans, emphasize oral learning traditions more than written ones, developing different skills, such as the basic understanding of story flow.

Factors Affecting Parents Who Are Immigrants to America

Parents educated in other countries may not know a great deal about the American educational system, and may not be aware of the educational demands made on their children, even in early childhood. Educators need to work with these parents to find common ground by identifying shared goals for children. While culturally diverse parents may disagree with some educators' goals, they can collaborate with educators to promote those on which they do agree. Immigrant parents may also be unaware of additional services available in America for children with developmental and/or learning problems. Educators can help parents by providing this information. Another consideration is that some other cultures have more paternalistic educational systems. Parents from such cultures, rather than vocally advocating for their children who need services, tend to wait for teachers/specialists to voice concerns before communicating any problems they have observed. Thus, they could miss out on the chance to obtain helpful services. Even worse, educators could misconstrue their behavior as a lack of interest in children's progress, or as resistance to confronting problems.

Developmental Milestones Varying by Culture

Research has found that different cultures have different age expectations for many early childhood developmental milestones. For example, Filipinos expect children to eat using utensils at 32.4 months. Anglo families expect children to do this at 17.7 months, and Puerto Ricans expect children to reach this milestone at 26.5 months. Filipino cultures expect children to sleep all night by 32.4 months; Puerto Rican and Anglo cultures expect this at 14.5 and 14.4 months, respectively. Similarly, while Anglos expect children to sleep by themselves at around 13.8 months and Puerto Ricans at around 14.6 months, Filipinos do not expect this until 38.8 months. Filipinos expect children to eat solid food by 6.7 months; Anglos by 8.2 months; and Puerto Ricans by 10.1 months. In Anglo families, an 18-month-old not drinking from a cup could indicate developmental delay if parents introduced the cup when s/he was one year old and regularly continued encouraging cup use. But, Filipino parents of an 18-month-old have likely not even introduced the child to a cup yet, so the fact that the child is not using a cup would not be cause for concern from a development standpoint.

When EC researchers investigated the average expectations of different cultural groups of when children would reach various developmental milestones, some of the milestones they examined included: eating solid food, weaning from nursing, drinking from a cup, eating with the fingers, eating with utensils, sleeping alone, sleeping through the night, choosing one's own clothes, dressing oneself, and playing alone. They also looked at daytime and nighttime toilet training.

Educators must become aware of different cultures' different socialization goals before assuming culturally diverse children have developmental delays. On the other hand, they must also avoid automatically attributing variations in milestone achievement to cultural child rearing differences when full developmental assessments might be indicated. Family expectations and values influence the complex process of developmental assessment. When families and assessors share common cultures, it is more likely that valid data will be collected and interpreted. When their cultures differ, however, it is more likely that the assessment information will be misinterpreted. Employing EC teachers/care providers who are familiar with the child, family, and assessment setting as mediators can make developmental assessments more culturally competent.

Essential Geographical Concepts

Ten concepts considered essential to the study of geography are: location, distance, achievability, pattern, morphology, agglomeration, utility value, interaction, area differentiation, and spatial interrelatedness. (1) Location: This concept identifies "where" a place is and examines the positive and negative properties of any place on the surface of the Earth. Absolute location is based upon latitude and longitude. Relative location is based upon changing characteristics of a region, and is influenced by surrounding areas. For example, urban areas have higher land prices than rural ones. (2) Distance: This identifies "how far" a place is, and is often described in terms of location. It is also related to the effort required to meet basic life needs. For example, the distance of raw materials from factories affects transportation costs and hence product prices. In another example, land costs less the farther it is from highways. (3) Achievability: The conditions on the Earth's surface dictate how accessible a geographic area is. For example, villages on beaches are easier to reach. Villages surrounded by forests or swamps are harder to reach. As its economy, science, technology, and transportation develop, a region's level of dependency on other areas changes.

(4) Patterns These are found in geographical forms and in how geographical phenomena spread, which affect dependency on those phenomena. For example, in fold regions (areas where the folding of rocks forms mountains), the rivers typically form trellis patterns. Patterns are also seen in human activity that is based on geography. For example, in mountainous regions, settlements predominantly form spreading patterns. (5) Morphology This is the shape of our planet's surface resulting from inner and outer forces. For example, along the northern coast of Java, sugarcane plantations predominate on the lowlands. (6) Agglomeration This is defined as collecting into a mass, and refers to a geographic concentration of people, activities, and/or settlements within areas that are most profitable and relatively narrow in size. (7) Utility value This refers to the existence and relative usefulness of natural resources. For example, fishermen find more utility value in the ocean than farmers do, and naturalists perceive more utility value in forests than academics would.

(8) Interaction This is the reciprocal and interdependent relationship between two or more geographical areas, which can generate new geographical phenomena, configurations, and problems. For example, a rural village produces raw materials through activities like mining ores or growing and harvesting plant crops, while a city produces industrial goods. The village needs the city as a market for its raw materials, and may also need the city's industrial products. The city needs the village for its raw materials to use in industrial production. This interdependence causes interaction. (9) Area differentiation This informs the study of variations among regional geographical phenomena. For example, different plants are cultivated in highlands vs. lowlands due to their different altitudes and climates. Area differentiation also informs the study of regional variations in occupation (farming vs. fishing, etc.). (10) Spatial interrelatedness This shows the relationship between/among geographic and non-physical phenomena, like rural and urban areas. The example above of village-city interaction also applies here.

Geographical Maps

General Features and Purposes

Maps can be drawn to show natural or man-made features. For example, some maps depict mountains, elevations (altitudes), average rainfall, average temperatures, and other natural features of an area. Other maps are made to depict countries, states, cities, roads, empires, wars, and other man-made features. Some maps include both natural and man-made features (e.g., a map showing a certain country and its elevations). Different types of maps are described according to their purposes. For example, political maps are made to depict countries, areas within a country, and/or cities. Physical maps are drawn to display natural features of the terrain in an area, such as rivers, lakes, and mountains. Thematic maps are drawn to focus on a more specific theme or topic, such as the locations and names of battles during a war or the average amounts of rainfall a country, state, or region receives in a given year or month. Some maps are made for more than one purpose, and indicate more than one of the types of information described above.

Basic Tools Supplied on Maps

On maps depicting local, national, and world geography, cartographers supply tools for navigating these maps. For example, the compass rose indicates the directions of north, south, east, and west. By looking at the compass, people can identify the locational relationships of places (e.g., in South America, Chile is west of Argentina). The scale of miles indicates how distances on a map correspond to actual geographical distances, enabling us to estimate real distances. For example, the scale might show that one inch is equal to 500 miles. By placing a piece of paper on the map, we can mark it to measure the distance between two cities (e.g., Washington, DC, in the USA and Ottawa in Canada) on the map, and then line the paper up with the scale of miles to estimate an actual distance of approximately 650 miles between the two cities. Map keys/legends identify what a map's symbols and colors represent.

Grids

Maps show absolute geographic location (i.e. the precise "address" of any place on the planet) using a grid of lines. The lines running from east to west are called parallels or latitudes, and they correspond to how many degrees away from the equator a place is located. The lines running from north to south are called meridians or longitudes, and they correspond to how many degrees away from the prime meridian a place is located. To determine the absolute location of a place, we find the spot on the map where its latitude and longitude intersect. This intersection is the place's absolute location. For example, if we look at Mexico City on a map, we will find that its latitude is 19° north and its longitude is 99° west, which is expressed in cartography as 19° N, 99° W. Numbers of latitudes and longitudes like these are also referred to as coordinates.

Reading and Analyzing a Special Purpose Map

(1) First, read a map's title and look at the overall map. This provides a general idea of what the map shows. For example, a map entitled "Battles of the Punic Wars" would not be a good choice if someone was looking for the political boundaries of modern day Greece, Italy, and Spain. (2) Next, read the map's legend/key to see what symbols and colors the map uses, and what each represents. For example, some lines represent divisions between countries/states; some, roads; some, rivers; etc. Different colors can indicate different countries/states, elevations, amounts of rainfall, population densities, etc. These are not uniform across all maps, so legends/keys are necessary references. (3) Use the legend/key to interpret what the map shows. For example, by looking at colors representing elevations, one can determine which area of a country has the highest/lowest altitude. (4) Draw conclusions about what the map displays. For example, if a country map mainly

has one color that indicates a certain elevation range, it can be concluded that this is the country's most common elevation.

Graphs

Graphs display numerical information in pictorial forms, making it easier to view statistics quickly and draw conclusions about them. For example, it is easier to see patterns/trends like increases/decreases in quantities using visual graphs than columns of numbers. Line graphs, bar graphs, and pie charts are the most common types of graphs. Line graphs depict changes over time by plotting points for a quantity measured each day/week/month/year/decade/century etc. and connecting the points to make a line. For example, showing the population of a city/country each decade in a line graph reveals how the population has risen/fallen/both. Bar graphs compare quantities related to different times/places/people/things. Each quantity is depicted by a separate bar, and its height/length corresponds to a number. Bar graphs make it easy to see which amounts are largest/smallest within a group (e.g., which of several cities/countries has the largest population). Pie charts/circle graphs divide a circle/"pie" into segments/"slices" showing percentages/parts of a whole, which also facilitates making comparisons. For example, the city/country with the largest population is the largest segment on a pie chart or circle graph.

Review Video: Bar Graph
Visit mometrix.com/academy and enter code: 226729

Review Video: Line Graphs
Visit mometrix.com/academy and enter code: 480147

Review Video: Pie Chart
Visit mometrix.com/academy and enter code: 895285

Review Video: Identifying Units and Trends in a Chart
Visit mometrix.com/academy and enter code: 638347

Importance of Chronological Thinking to Understanding History

To see cause-and-effect relationships in historical events and explore and understand relationships among those events, students must have a solid grasp of when things happened and in what time sequence (chronology). Teachers can help students develop chronological thinking by using and assigning well-constructed/well-written narratives. These include histories written in the same style as stories, works of historical literature, and biographies. These hold students' attention, allowing them to focus on authors' depictions of temporal relationships among antecedents, actions, and consequences; of historical motivations and deeds of individuals and groups; and of the time structure of sequential occurrences. By middle school, students should have the skills needed to measure time mathematically (e.g., in years/decades/centuries/millennia), interpret data displayed in timelines, and calculate time in BCE and CE. High school students should be able to analyze patterns of historical duration (e.g., how long the U.S. Constitutional government has lasted) and patterns of historical succession (e.g., the development of expanding trade and communication systems, from Neolithic times through ancient empires and from early modern times to modern global interaction).

Educational Standards That Demonstrate Skills in Historical and Chronological Thinking

Students should be able to differentiate among past, present, and future. They should be able to identify the beginning, middle, and end/outcome of historical narratives/stories. They also should be able to construct their own historical narratives, including working forward and backward in time from some event to explain causes and temporal development of various events, issues, etc. Students should be able to calculate and measure calendar time, including days/dates, weeks, months, years, centuries, and millennia. They should be able to describe time periods using BCE/BC and CE/AD. They should be skilled at comparing calendar systems (e.g., Roman, Gregorian, Julian, Hebrew, Muslim, Mayan, and others) and at relating the calendar years of major historical events. They should be able to look at timelines and interpret the information they contain, and make their own timelines using equidistant time intervals and recording events sequentially. Students should be able to explain change and continuity in history through reconstructing and applying patterns of historical duration and succession. They should be able to identify the structural principles that are the bases of alternative periodization models, and to compare these models.

Reasons/Purposes for Our Country's Laws and Teaching Citizenship

Young children must understand the purposes of rules/laws: They identify acceptable/unacceptable citizen behaviors; make society and life predictable, secure, and orderly; designate responsibilities to citizens; and prevent persons in authority positions from abusing their roles by limiting their power. Understanding these functions of laws/rules enables children to realize that our government consists of individuals and groups authorized to create, implement, and enforce laws and manage legal disputes. Some creative EC teachers have used children's literature to illustrate these concepts. Children can relate personally to stories' characters, and story situations make the concepts real and concrete to children. Stories can be springboards for discussing rules and when they do/do not apply. One activity involves children in small groups making class rules (e.g., "No talking" and "Stay in your seat"), and then rewriting these to be more realistic (e.g., "Talk softly in class; listen when others talk" and "Sit down and get right to work"). Children consider issues of safety and fairness, and develop an understanding of judicial and legislative roles.

Human Health and Wellness and Disease Prevention

Health and disease prevention begin before birth. Expecting mothers need to be/become informed about good nutrition for all humans and the supplemental nutrition required for prenatal support of developing embryos and fetuses. Mothers also need to get sufficient but not overly strenuous exercise; avoid undue stress; have/learn effective coping skills to deal with unavoidable life stressors; and avoid exposure to environmental toxins, such as radiation, pollution, and chemicals. They should avoid alcohol, tobacco, and exposure to secondhand smoke, as well as most drugs—street, over-the-counter, herbal, and prescription—unless they are prescribed by obstetricians/other physicians who are aware of the pregnancy. Babies initially need their mother's colostrum to provide immunity, and subsequently require breast milk or approved infant formula. Babies must also be held, cuddled, and given attention and affection to ensure survival, growth, and health. Young children need smaller amounts of food than adults that is equally as nutritious; sufficient exercise; adequate sleep; and cognitive, emotional, and social stimulation and interaction. Appropriate nutrition and exercise, avoidance of alcohol/tobacco/other drugs, and positive relationships and interactions are essential for wellness and disease prevention at all ages.

2009 American Recovery and Reinvestment Act

The 2009 American Recovery and Reinvestment Act has allotted $650 million for preventing chronic disease. To apply these funds, the U.S. Department of Health and Human Services (HHS) has designed a comprehensive initiative entitled Communities Putting Prevention to Work. This initiative aims to create sustainable positive health changes in American communities, prevent or delay chronic disease, reduce disease risk factors, and promote child and adult wellness. Obesity and tobacco use, considered the foremost preventable sources of disability and death, are targeted by this initiative's evidence-based research programs and strategies, which are intended to reinforce state abilities and mobilize community resources. The initiative's central, $373-million community program includes support from the Centers for Disease Control and Prevention in selected communities for attaining the prevention outcomes of increasing physical activity levels, improving nutrition, reducing the incidence of obesity and higher than optimal body weights, decreasing tobacco use, and decreasing secondhand smoke exposure. Through this initiative, HHS hopes to produce effective models that can be reproduced in states and communities nationwide.

Environmental Health Risks

Children's body systems, unlike those of mature adults, are still developing. They eat, drink, and breathe more in proportion to their body sizes than adults do. Typical child behaviors expose children to more potentially toxic chemicals and organisms. Therefore, children can be more vulnerable to environmental health risks. To protect children, adults can prohibit smoking in homes and cars; keep homes free of dust, mold, pet dander, and pests that can trigger allergies; avoid outdoor activities on high-pollution/"ozone alert" days; and carpool and/or use public transportation. Adults can prevent lead poisoning by only giving children cold water to drink and using cold water to prepare infant formula and cook food; washing bottles, pacifiers, and toys frequently; and protecting children from lead-based paints in older buildings. Adults must ensure children do not have access to toxic chemicals. Maintaining furnaces, chimneys, and appliances; using outdoor gas appliances and tools properly; refraining from using gas appliances and tools indoors; and installing approved CO alarms can all help prevent carbon monoxide poisoning. Choosing fish carefully can help prevent mercury toxicity. Keeping infants out of direct sunlight, using sun-protective clothing, and applying sunscreen on young children are also important.

Federal Executive Order 13045: Protection of Children from Environmental Health Risks and Safety Risks (1997)

Passed by President Clinton, Executive Order 13045 declares a policy for identifying and assessing environmental health and safety risks that affect children disproportionately, and for addressing these risks through the policies, standards, programs, and activities of every independent federal regulatory agency. This order defines environmental health and safety risks as those that can be attributed to substances children ingest or contact (e.g., air they breathe; food they eat; water they drink, bathe in, and swim in; soil they live upon; and products they are exposed to or use). The order established a task force reporting to the president and consulting with the Domestic Policy Council, the National Science and Technology Council, the Council on Environmental Quality, and the Office of Management and Budget. The task force is co-chaired by the HHS secretary and the EPA administrator. The task force oversees a coordinated, integrated federal research agenda and reports relevant research/data biennially; issues principle, policy, and priority statements; recommends appropriate federal/state/local/tribal government, nonprofit, and private sector partnerships; makes public outreach/communication proposals; identifies related high-priority initiatives; and evaluates new legislation to determine whether it will meet the goals of Executive Order 13045.

Circulatory System

The circulatory system continuously supplies blood containing oxygen and nutrients to all body tissue cells, exchanges oxygenated blood for the waste products produced during the metabolism process, and transports waste for elimination. Central to the vascular (vessel) system is the heart, which is located in the mediastinum within the thoracic cavity. The heart is encased and protected by the pericardium, a double-walled, tough fibrous sac. The heart has four chambers: two atria and two ventricles. A system of valves regulates opening/closing among the chambers, the aorta, the pulmonary artery, and the great vessels. The aorta, originating at the heart, is the body's largest artery. The pulmonary artery branches to the left and to the right, and transports venous blood from the heart's lower right chamber to the lung for oxygenation. The pulmonary veins return oxygenated blood from the lung to the left atrium of the heart. The superior and inferior venae cavae are vessels that empty into the heart's right atrium.

Integumentary and Musculoskeletal Systems

In the human body, the integumentary system consists of skin, hair, nails, and oil and sweat glands. The skin has three layers: the epidermis, the dermis, and subcutaneous tissues. Skin protects tissues underneath it from bacterial infections, blocks most chemicals from entering, prevents fluid loss, and reduces the probability of mechanical injury to underlying body structures. Skin regulates body temperature and synthesizes needed chemicals. It is also a sense organ, as it has sensory receptors for touch, pressure, heat/cold, and pain. It also contains motor fibers that enable necessary reactions to these sensations and stimuli. The musculoskeletal system includes bones, joints, and connective tissues: tendons, ligaments, and cartilage. It is responsible for our body shape, and provides stability and support. It also protects our internal organs and enables locomotion. Bones store calcium and other minerals, and bone marrow produces required blood cells. Muscle fibers contract to enable movement. Depending on their innervation, muscles can have voluntary or involuntary (like the heart) movements. Muscles need blood supply and oxygen to work. Thus, the musculoskeletal system depends on other systems, including the circulatory, nervous, and respiratory systems.

Lymphatic System

The lymphatic system includes lymph (a fluid), collection ducts, and tissues. Lymphatic tissues comprise the lymph nodes, the thymus gland, the tonsils, and the Peyer's patches of the intestinal tract. Lymphoid components are also present in the lungs, the mucosa in the stomach and the appendix, and the bone marrow. Microscopic capillaries merge to form lymph-collecting ducts. These ducts drain to specific centers of lymphatic tissue. The lymph system's functioning is supported by the spleen and thymus glands. While not all characteristics and functions of the lymphatic system are established, known functions include: return transportation of lymph, protein, and microorganisms to the cardiovascular system; production of lymphocytes by the lymph nodes; filtering of the blood by the lymph nodes; production of antibodies to enable immune response against infection; absorption of fats and fat soluble substances from the intestine; formation of blood cells in response to some illnesses/conditions; and phagocytosis (i.e. the surrounding/swallowing/"eating" of infectious particles by cells lining the sinuses of the lymph nodes, spleen, and liver). The lymph system defends the body against infection and supports the veins by helping to return fluids to the bloodstream.

Respiratory System

The respiratory system provides oxygen to the body and removes carbon dioxide, the waste product of respiration (breathing). In doing so, the respiratory system and many other body systems work together through complex interactions. Twelve thoracic vertebrae, twelve pairs of ribs, the sternum, the diaphragm, and the intercostal muscles comprise the thoracic cage containing the lungs. As one breathes in and out, the thoracic cage is always moving. The diaphragm, a muscular wall dividing the chest cavity and abdominal cavity, functions as a bellows for breathing. (It also plays a role in expelling feces and delivering babies.) There are air pathways between the nose/mouth, pharynx, trachea, bronchi, bronchioles, and lungs. Alveoli, tiny air sacs in the lungs, exchange oxygen and carbon dioxide. During inspiration/inhalation, the ribs and sternum rise, the diaphragm contracts and lowers, the intercostal muscles contract, air pressure in the lungs decreases, and air enters the lungs. During exhalation, the intercostal muscles and diaphragm relax, the ribs and sternum return to a resting position, air pressure in the lungs increases, and air exits the lungs.

The Brain

The brain is divided into five major parts: the cerebrum, the midbrain, the cerebellum, the pons, and the medulla oblongata. The cranial nerves are: I – olfactory, which controls the sense of smell; II – optic, which controls vision; III – oculomotor, which controls the movements of the eye muscles, the movements of the upper eyelids, and the pupillary reflexes (expanding and contracting to admit more/less light); IV – trochlear, which controls the movements of the superior oblique eye muscles; V – trigeminal, which controls facial sensation, the eye's corneal reflex, and chewing; VI – abducens, which controls the movements of the lateral rectus eye muscle; VII – facial, which controls movement of the facial muscles and the taste sensation in the front two-thirds of the tongue; VIII – vestibulocochlear, which controls equilibrium (balance) via the vestibular system in the inner ear, and hearing (the cochlea is in the inner ear); IX – glossopharyngeal, which controls the taste sensation in the rear one-third of the tongue; X – vagus, which controls pharyngeal contraction (gag reflex), vocal cord movements, and soft palate movements; XI – spinal accessory, which controls movement of the sternocleidomastoid and trapezius muscles; and XII – hypoglossal, which controls tongue movements.

Central Nervous System

Some main functions of the central nervous system (i.e. the brain and spinal cord) include controlling consciousness and all mental processes, regulating the functions and movements of the body, and sending and receiving nerve impulses to and from all parts of the body. For example, when we touch something hot, sensory nerve endings in our fingers send impulses to the brain, which interprets them as heat and sends a signal along motor nerves to pull our fingers away. The autonomic nervous system is automatic and involuntary. For example, it makes our heart beat. We cannot voluntarily start/stop our heartbeat. The voluntary nervous system is under our conscious control. For example, our brains use it to send impulses to our skeletal muscles when we want to sit/stand/walk, etc., which contract in response. The autonomic nervous system is divided into parasympathetic and sympathetic components. The parasympathetic portion stimulates muscular activity in the organs and gland secretion. The sympathetic portion stimulates heartbeat, vasoconstriction, and sweating. These two portions of the autonomic nervous system oppose/balance each other to regulate system

Digestive System

The chief functions of the digestive system are to provide nutrition to the body's cells and eliminate waste products left after nourishment is extracted from foods. The process consists of three phases: ingestion (i.e. taking in foods and liquids), digestion (i.e. converting ingested nutrients through physical and chemical means into forms that the cells of the body tissues can absorb and distribute), and elimination (i.e. removing the byproducts of digestion—also known as waste—that cannot be utilized). Other body systems work with the digestive system to process nutrients. For example, the nervous system plays a role in appetite, which is a signal for us to eat. The central nervous system also stimulates the release and flow of digestive juices. The endocrine system supplies chemicals (e.g., juices from the pancreas) that aid in digestion. The circulatory system delivers digested and absorbed nutrients to the tissue cells, and also picks up waste products produced as a result of the metabolism process.

During chewing, our teeth and tongue physically break down food. Glands secrete saliva to provide lubrication during chewing and swallowing, and provide digestive enzymes to begin the process of chemically breaking down the foods we eat. The pharynx delivers food to the esophagus, where muscular contractions (peristalsis) move food downward. The epiglottis closes the trachea (windpipe) during swallowing to prevent food from being aspirated into the lungs. Glands in the stomach lining secrete gastric fluid comprised of hydrochloric acid and other chemicals, which dissolve food into semiliquid chyme. Chyme gradually passes into the small intestine, where most digestion and absorption occur. The small intestine is made up of the duodenum, the jejunum, and the ileum. The pancreas secretes digestive juices, the gallbladder secretes bile, and the intestinal mucosa secretes other juices into the duodenum to digest chyme. Digested nutrients are absorbed through the intestinal walls into capillaries and lymphatic vessels to be distributed to body cells. The large intestine consists of the cecum, the colon (ascending, transverse, descending, and sigmoid), the rectum, and the anus. The colon completes digestion and absorption, and delivers wastes to the rectum, which eliminates them through the anus.

Urinary System

The function of the urinary system is to eliminate the liquid wastes produced through nutrient metabolism by excreting them from the body. The urinary system is made up of two kidneys, two ureters, the bladder, and the urethra. Behind the abdominal cavity at the thoraco-lumbar level are the kidneys, a pair of large bean-shaped glands. They continually remove water, salts, toxins, and nitrogenous wastes from the bloodstream, and convert these substances into urine. Urine droplets flow from the kidneys into the ureters. The ureters are long, narrow tubes carrying urine to the bladder, which is a hollow, muscular, elastic organ. When enough urine collects in the bladder, nerves stimulate the body to empty it via urination. In human females, the urethra is about an inch and a half long, and is located in the upper vaginal wall. In males, the urethra is about eight inches long, and extends from the bladder through the prostate gland and the penis. Both urine and sperm pass through the male urethra, while the female urethra and vaginal canal are separate.

Endocrine System

The human endocrine system is one of the most complex body systems. Scientists understand many of its functions, but not all of them. It is a system of ductless, internally secreting glands (some necessary to life) that extract various substances from tissue fluids and the bloodstream to create completely new substances (i.e. hormones). Operating without ducts, endocrine glands secrete hormones directly into the blood and lymph circulatory systems for distribution to the organs. The endocrine system's main glands include the pituitary, thyroid, parathyroid, and adrenal glands; the

Islets of Langerhans in the pancreas; and the gonads (male testes and female ovaries). Additionally, the pancreas is both an endocrine and an exocrine gland. Its endocrine (internal secretion) function is to secrete insulin to regulate sugar metabolism; its exocrine (external secretion) function is to secrete pancreatic juice into the duodenum to aid in digestion. If the pancreas produces insufficient insulin, type 1 diabetes results. If the body responds insufficiently to insulin, type 2 diabetes results.

Pituitary, Thyroid, and Parathyroid Glands

The pituitary and thyroid glands are both components of the endocrine system. The pituitary gland functions directly by regulating physical growth, development, and sexual maturation in children and adolescents; regulating the retention and excretion of fluid; regulating the balance of electrolytes (sodium, potassium, and chloride) in blood and tissues; and regulating new mothers' lactation (milk production). The pituitary is termed the hypophyseal /"master gland" because it also regulates all other glands in the endocrine system. Therefore, it is involved in regulating food assimilation and metabolism through hydrating the thyroid gland; regulating body composition, adaptation, and resistance to stress through acting on the adrenal and parathyroid glands; regulating breathing, circulation, digestion, urine excretion, and muscular action through the collective activity of multiple hormones; and regulating sexual development, activity, and reproduction through acting on the gonads. The thyroid gland manufactures and secretes hormones that regulate child growth and development, as well as certain metabolic processes and their rates. It also stores iodine. The parathyroid glands secrete hormones that regulate blood calcium levels, phosphorus metabolism, and muscle and nervous system excitation.

Reproductive System

Male

The scrotum and the penis are the external reproductive organs of the human male. The internal organs of the male reproductive system include two testes, two epididymides, two seminal ducts, two seminal vesicles, two ejaculatory ducts, two spermatic cords, the urethra, the prostate gland, and several other glands. The testes, which are glandular organs, hang on either side of the scrotum from spermatic cords. These cords contain the vas deferens, blood vessels, and supportive tissues. Male sperm cells and hormones are produced by the testes. Each testis has an epididymis connecting it to the vas deferens, an excretory seminal duct. The vas deferens travel upward inside the spermatic cords to the prostate gland, which is in front of the neck of the urinary bladder. There, the vas deferens join with the pouch-like glands called seminal vesicles to form ejaculatory ducts. The prostate gland and seminal vesicles secrete substances into the semen that promote sperm motility. The ejaculatory ducts release semen into the urethra, and from here the semen is ejected through the penis during sexual intercourse.

Female

The external female reproductive organs include the mons pubis, the labia majora, the labia minora, the clitoris, the vestibule, the hymen, the Bartholin's glands, and several other glands. The breasts/mammary glands can also be considered parts of the reproductive system, as they produce milk for infants following reproduction. Internal organs include the vagina, the two fallopian tubes, the uterus, and the two ovaries. Hormones stimulate either ovary to produce an ovum/egg roughly once a month. A follicle containing an egg cell forms. When the egg matures, the follicle ruptures, releasing the egg. This is known as ovulation. The ovum passes into a fallopian tube and travels toward the uterus. Hormones have meanwhile also stimulated the endometrium (uterine lining) to thicken and increase its blood supply. When the egg reaches the womb, it is implanted in the endometrium if it was fertilized in the fallopian tube by a male sperm. This is known as conception. If the egg was not fertilized, hormone signals subside, causing the endometrium to detach from the uterine wall. The sloughed off endometrial tissue, the resulting blood, and the unfertilized egg exit the body. This process is known as menstruation.

Influence of Physical, Emotional, and Social Factors on Personal Physical Health

The parts of the body, including the brain, are connected, related, interactive, and interdependent. As humans also interact and are interdependent with their environment, both internal and external factors influence their health. For example, physical factors like exposure to air pollution or radiation can cause illnesses like asthma, other lung diseases, and various cancers. Too much or too little nutrition can cause obesity and diabetes* or malnutrition. Too much or too little exercise can cause exhaustion and injuries or weakness, diabetes*, and cardiovascular and pulmonary problems. Not exercising enough may also be a factor in being overweight or obese. *Diabetes itself causes many related health problems, including blindness, circulatory deficiencies, amputation, and cardiovascular disease. Water and/or sleep deprivation ultimately cause death. Emotional factors like depression, anxiety, and irritability can cause a host of health problems, including insomnia, overeating, anorexia, high blood pressure, and heart disease. Social factors include family influences. According to the family systems theory, dysfunctional family dynamics can cause a child to develop a physical illness. Whether the source is family, society outside the home, or both, stress is a social influence with multiple negative health impacts.

Effect of Nutrition on Development

Children must consume a full range of nutrients for their brains to work normally. They need protein for its amino acids, which enable the brain's neurotransmitters (chemical messengers) to fire and communicate with each other. They need fruit and vegetable sugars and other complex carbohydrates to supply fuel to power the brain's functioning. Children's nutrition begins before birth. Pregnant women who do not eat adequate nutrients, vitamins, and minerals have higher risks of delivering infants with low birth weights. Research has found that babies with low birth weights are more likely to experience hearing and vision problems, and to need special education services in school at some point. Children in school who consume insufficient amounts of protein have been found to score lower on achievement tests than their peers who are getting enough protein. Children with iron deficiencies display fatigue and ADHD-like symptoms, including impaired concentration, shortened attention spans, and irritability. Children who miss breakfast consistently perform slower on problem solving tests than those who do not. Their responses are also less accurate. Children who regularly miss meals have compromised immunity against illnesses and infections, and they miss more school.

Motor Skills

Motor skills are the large and small movements of the body. These movements include such things as pushing, pulling, lifting, and carrying larger objects using the legs, arms, and back; and picking up, grasping, and manipulating smaller objects using the hands and fingers. The former are gross motor skills, and the latter are fine motor skills. To develop these, children must make effective use of their mind-body connection (i.e. getting the muscles and bones to perform the movements the mind intends). They must also have developed spatial awareness (i.e. an accurate sense of the relationship between their bodies and the surrounding space and other bodies/objects). Teaching children to move large and small muscles in time to rhythmic songs helps develop motor skills. Teaching directions like up, down, clockwise, counterclockwise, etc. helps with motor planning development. When children find motor skills challenging to master, educators must provide them with frequent instruction, adequate re-teaching, and ample modeling that allows them to observe and imitate problematic movements.

Fine Motor Movements

Fine motor movements use small muscles in the eyes, lips, tongue, wrists, fingers, and toes. Fine/small motor movements work together with gross/large muscle movements to develop movement skills and patterns. Fine motor skills are often used for purposes of functional and expressive communication, like using tools, creating artworks, and writing and typing language. Eye-hand coordination, eye-foot coordination, and manual and finger dexterity are required for the fine motor movements used in drawing, writing, and typing. Fine motor practice also develops children's tactile (touch) awareness and spatial awareness. Rolling dough/putty/clay into balls and/or hiding things inside them promote fine motor skills. Tearing and cutting paper along dotted lines and creating patterns teach accurate size and shape perception and formation. Stringing, lacing, and creating structures using plastic building blocks develop hand-eye coordination and skills needed to create color patterns. Flip cards, pegs, and stickers promote object placement skills. Writing skills are developed by writing letters/numbers in shaving cream, sand, pudding, and/or on chalkboards using wet makeup sponges/cotton swabs; using toothbrushes on dry erase boards; and practicing placement on cardboard using rice, beans, wet/dry pasta, glitter, etc.

Newborn/Infant Motor Reflexes and Skills

Newborns exhibit the tonic reflex, adopting the "fencing position." In this position, the head is turned to one side, the arm on that side is in front of the eyes, and the other arm is flexed. This normally disappears by the time an infant is around four months old. It may serve as preparation for reaching voluntarily for things/people. The stepping reflex disappears at around two months of age, and prepares babies for walking voluntarily. The palmar grasping reflex on an adult finger disappears by the time an infant is around three to four months old, and prepares babies for grasping voluntarily. When held upright, a baby can typically hold his/her head steady and erect by about six weeks of age on average. About 90 percent of infants will develop this skill between the ages of three weeks and four months. Babies lift up from the prone position using their arms by the time they are about two months old. About 90 percent of infants will develop this skill between the ages of three weeks and four months. Babies can also roll from side to back by the time they are about two months old. About 90 percent of infants will develop this skill between the ages of three weeks and five months. An infant can grasp a cube by the age of three months and three weeks on average. About 90 percent of infants will develop this skill between the ages of two and seven months.

Gross Motor Skills

The first motor movements of EC are gross motor skills (i.e. large body movements involving the torso, limbs, and feet). Sitting, standing, crawling, walking, running, galloping, jumping, catching, throwing, and kicking use these skills. Activities that help young children develop their gross motor skills include standing on dots/marks on the floor/ground; crawling under and climbing over things, including objects that are part of obstacle courses; and balancing on balance beams. These develop body control, coordination, laterality (using the left/right sides of the body separately), and synchronization of the body's left and right sides. Children develop body control and balance through hopping around objects. They develop coordination and overall gross motor skills through jumping over things like boxes, beanbags, lines/strings; and by kicking balls, balloons, etc. of various sizes. Walking and running around, through, and/or over obstacles like tires, hoops, etc. and/or participating in relays develop gross motor skills. Organized games involving skipping around things to music with various rhythms, and activities requiring twisting, turning, and bending all develop gross motor skills, preparing children for lifelong engagement in sports activities.

How Cooking and Self-Care Activities Help Develop Fine Motor Skills

Young children are often fascinated by adults' cooking activities, want to participate, and offer to help. Involving them is not only beneficial to their self-esteem, but also develops various skills. Measuring amounts of liquids and solids in different forms develops children's math skills. Mixing, stirring, and blending ingredients using different parts of their hands develop children's fine motor skills. Life skills include self-care skills, such as combing one's hair, brushing one's teeth, fastening and unfastening buttons and snaps on clothing, and lacing and unlacing shoes. Life skills also require being able to open and close drawers, doors, and jars; to clean a house; and to wash things. It is necessary to children's normal development that they learn to combine multiple fine motor skills. Children's development of fine motor skills also needs to be integrated with the development of various self-care and other life skills (such as those described above) that are required for normal activities of daily living.

Infant Motor Skills Milestones

By four and a half months on average, babies can roll from back to side. The range within which 90 percent of infants will be able to do this is two to seven months. Most babies can sit unsupported by seven months on average. The range within which 90 percent of infants will be able to do this is five to nine months. Most infants also crawl by seven months on average. The range within which 90 percent of infants will be able to do this is five to eleven months. Babies pull themselves up to a standing position by around eight months on average. The range within which 90 percent of infants will be able to do this is five to twelve months. Babies play "patty-cake" by nine months, three weeks on average. The range within which 90 percent of infants will be able to do this is seven to fifteen months. Babies/toddlers can stand alone by 11 months on average. The range within which 90 percent of infants will be able to do this is 9 to 16 months. Toddlers can walk unassisted by the age of 11 months, 3 weeks on average. The range within which 90 percent of infants will be able to do this is 9 to 17 months. Children can stack two cubes by the age of 13 months, 3 weeks on average. The range within which 90 percent of infants will be able to do this is 10 to 19 months. They scribble energetically by the age of 14 months on average. The range within which 90 percent of infants will be able to do this is 10 to 21 months. They can climb stairs with assistance by the age of 16 months on average. The range within which 90 percent of infants will be able to do this is 12 to 23 months. Normally developing children can typically can jump in place by the age of 23 months, 2 weeks on average. The range within which 90 percent of infants will be able to do this is 17 to 30 months.

Cephalocaudal and Proximodistal Development

Infant and child motor development follows the same developmental sequences as prenatal embryonic and fetal physical development. Cephalocaudal means head to tail. Just as the body develops from the head down before birth, babies and young children develop motor control of their heads before they develop control of their legs. Proximodistal means near to far (i.e. central to distant). Head, torso, and arm control develop before hand and finger control. Babies learn a lot about how things look, sound, and feel once they master gross motor skills for reaching and grasping. These then evolve toward fine motor skills. For example, at around three months of age an infant's voluntary reaching gradually becomes more accurate. The infant will not need arm guidance, because he or she has spatial awareness of location and motion. Babies reach less by five months when they can move things within reach. By nine months, babies can redirect reaching to grasp objects moving in different directions. By six to twelve months, development of the pincer grasp enhances babies' capacities for object manipulation.

Benefits of Physical Activity

When young children engage in physical activity, they learn new motor skills and reinforce, advance, and refine existing ones. They also learn important early math skills like spatial awareness. Whenever they attempt new activities, they encounter challenges, such as having to develop higher levels of coordination, control, precision, strength, speed, flexibility, and agility. They are also challenged to coordinate their mental and physical processes more closely and in a manner that is more complex. They learn to exert effort, and to persevere in the face of difficulty. When they succeed at meeting these challenges, their self-esteem and self-efficacy (sense of competence to perform tasks) are enhanced. Since motor skills generally develop ahead of language skills, physical activity is a valuable means of direct self-expression. Young children learn many social skills through interacting with peers and adults during physical games, sports activities, etc. In addition to all these benefits, young children normally seek out physical activity, deriving a great deal of fun and enjoyment through moving, playing games/sports, and interacting physically with others.

National Physical Education Standards

The National Association for Sport and Physical Education (NASPE) has developed six national physical education standards. These standards state that someone who is physically educated: (1) shows the motor skills and patterns of movement competencies s/he needs to conduct various physical activities; (2) shows comprehension of the basic concepts, main principles, methods, and techniques of movement as they relate to learning and executing physical activities; (3) regularly engages in physical activity; (4) reaches and sustains a level of physical fitness that enhances health; (5) demonstrates behaviors, personally and socially, that reflect self-respect and respect for others within contexts of physical activity; and (6) places value upon the benefits of physical activities and of being fit and active, such as the pleasure; the improvement and maintenance of health; the physical, personal, and social challenges; and the opportunities to interact socially and express oneself.

Motor Skills Developing Between Ages 2 and 6

Children develop motor skills most quickly between the ages of two and six years. They demonstrate basic locomotion skills, first walking and then running, skipping, hopping, galloping, and jumping. They also develop ball-handling skills, fine motor eye-hand coordination, and—as an extension of previously developed creeping skills—climbing skills. By two years of age, children develop balance for basic kicking, which evolves into the ability to execute full kicks (including backswings) by six years of age. They try throwing by two to three years of age. They develop related skills—including taking a forward step—by the age of six. They develop the ability to shuffle by three years of age, which develops into the ability to skip by six years of age. By the age of three, children walk automatically. They try running, but they are clumsy and lack adequate control. This ability improves by between four and five years of age. By this time, children are also more skilled at executing starts, stops, and turns. By the age of five or six, children can run like adults. They develop climbing skills (ladders, etc.) between the ages of three and six. The ability to jump longer distances and hopping and galloping skills develop by age six. Children can catch a large ball while holding their arm straight by the age of three. They can catch a ball while holding their elbows out to the front by age four, and they can do this while holding their elbows at their sides by age six.

Physical, Emotional, and Social Factors

Young children who have already become overweight/obese because of an improper diet and lack of exercise are more likely than children who are within a healthy weight range to find physical activity uncomfortable and avoid it. Even those who enjoy activity are more at risk of injury if they are overweight or lack physical conditioning. Exercise is more challenging for children with illnesses. For example, asthma interferes with breathing. Therefore, asthmatic children must be supervised and monitored when exercising. So must diabetic children, whose blood sugar can fluctuate excessively due to exercising. Their food intake must be monitored and coordinated with exercise. Children with physical disabilities may require adaptive equipment and/or alternative methods of physical instruction and exercising. Emotionally, children experiencing depression are likely to be apathetic and uninterested in movement. Hyperactive children (e.g., those with ADHD) are often overactive physically to the point of exhaustion. Children lacking adequate social skills, friends, and/or peer groups have fewer opportunities and are less likely to engage in physical games and sports with others, so their motor skills and physical fitness may suffer.

Amounts and Proportions of Engagement in Physical Activity

The World Health Organization (WHO) advises that children between the ages of 5 and 17 should engage in a minimum of 1 hour (continuously or incrementally) of moderate to vigorous physical activity per day. According to the World Health Organization, exercising for more than one hour daily (within reason) will confer additional health benefits. The majority of children's physical activity should be aerobic in nature. Aerobic exercise uses large muscle groups, is rhythmic and continuous, and works the heart and lungs so that the pulmonary and cardiovascular systems become more efficient at absorbing and transporting oxygen. Children should take part in exercises and/or activities that strengthen the muscles and bones through weight bearing and other methods at least three times per week. Children's play activities that can fulfill bone-strengthening requirements include running, jumping, turning, and playing various games. Engaging in general play, playing games, playing sports, doing chores, using exercise as a means of transportation (e.g., walking, biking, etc.), participating in planned exercise sessions, and attending physical education classes are all activities available in family, community, and school settings that can allow children to meet physical activity and fitness requirements.

Learning Outcomes Achieved Through Visual Arts

The arts are just as important to include in curricula as language, math, science, social studies, health, and physical education. Early learning standards in many states now reflect the goal to integrate the arts into the overall curriculum. Teachers need to provide young children with activities that promote development of fine motor skills, exploration of art materials and processes, and symbolic representation of concepts through artworks. EC educators should not merely assign isolated art activities. They can clarify many concepts and improve learning by providing art projects that fit into the overall curriculum and are relevant to individual learning units. Teachers should develop detailed, well-organized step lists for each activity. Clear directions not only maintain classroom order, but also provide children with a structure within which to experiment with art and enhance their sequencing skills. Teachers should use process-oriented activities, both on their own and within lessons that require products. For example, painting pictures of animals combines product (representing an animal) with process (exploring paint use). Teachers should supply and explain rules/steps for process activities that explore the use of art materials and processes.

Planning Art Activities or Projects

EC teachers should first establish the concept they want to teach, the objectives they want to meet through planning and teaching the lesson/activity, and the learning objectives they want the children to meet through participating. Then, a teacher can construct a simple prototype for the project. This enables the teacher to estimate how long it will take the children to complete the activity, and to explore and discover the optimal sequencing of steps for the activity. The teacher should then write down the plan, step-by-step. Steps should include those that need to be completed before the activity. These might include preliminary discussion, book reading/sharing related to the project, viewing related artworks and/or photos, etc. Steps should also include those that need to be completed while setting up the activity, such as dispensing paints, clay, etc.; assembling paintbrushes/other instruments; and passing out paper and other materials. Teachers do not need to be artistically proficient. Young children are not art critics, and teachers can find a great deal of information about art materials and processes by reading books and searching online. Available professional development courses focusing on art can also give teachers more ideas for lesson plans.

Functions of Art

<u>Social Functions</u>

Artworks can be created for physical, social, and personal purposes. When art focuses on the social lives of groups rather than on one individual's experiences or viewpoint, it serves social functions. Art carrying political stances/messages always performs social functions. Dadaist Oppenheim's hair-covered tea set did not perform any physical function, but served social functions by politically protesting World War I and many other social/political issues. During the Great Depression, photographers like Dorothea Lange, Gordon Parks, Walker Evans, and Arthur Rothstein commissioned by the Farm Security Administration produced stark records of people's suffering. These depictions of social conditions also served social functions. Fine artists like Francisco Goya and William Hogarth, as well as cartoonists like Thomas Nast and Charles Bragg, created satirical works of art lampooning various social and political customs and situations. Satire is intended not only to provide comic relief, insight, and perspective, but also to stimulate social change. Therefore, it serves social functions. Another social function is improving community status and pride through art treasures.

<u>Physical Functions</u>

Ascertaining the function of a work of art requires considering its context. Half of the context involves the artist. Knowing the artist's country, the historical time period during which the artist lived, and the social and political culture of the time informs artwork and our ability to infer what the artist was thinking and intending when he or she was creating it. The other half of the context involves the viewer. Knowing what the artwork means to you in your own place and time informs your perception of and response to it. Taken within context, art serves physical, personal, and social functions. For example, architecture, industrial design, and crafts have physical functions. A raku pottery bowl made in Japan serves a physical function during a tea ceremony. However, a teacup covered with hair (paired with a hair-covered saucer and spoon) by Dada artist Meret Oppenheim (1936) makes an artistic statement, but serves no physical function. When we view a tribal war club in a museum, regardless of the exquisite craftsmanship it may demonstrate, we realize it was made primarily for bludgeoning enemies.

Personal Functions

Works of art can have physical, social, and personal functions. Of these three, the personal functions of art are the most variable. Artists' motivations to create works include the desire to express their feelings and ideas, to obtain gratification through producing art, to communicate messages to viewers, to enable both themselves and their viewers to have an aesthetic experience, and to simply entertain viewers. Some artists also claim that they sometimes create art for no particular reason, and that the art produced has no meaning. Art can perform a personal function of control. For example, some artists use their work to give order to the world's apparent chaos. Others use art to create chaos in an overly orderly, boring environment. Art can be therapeutic for both artists and viewers. Much art has served the personal function of religion. Artworks with biological purposes, like cultural fertility symbols or bodily decorations designed to attract mates for procreation, are also examples of the personal functions of art.

Learning Objectives

When children participate in teacher-designed art activities, they can fulfill learning objectives such as exploring various art materials and processes; developing awareness of visual art and its basic elements (e.g., line, shape, color, and texture); using art forms to represent feelings, thoughts, and/or stories; developing the skills of color recognition and discrimination; and even building their vocabularies and language skills, depending on the activities. Teachers can integrate such objectives with an overall theme for each art activity/project that they integrate with the current theme for their lesson or curriculum unit. For example, if space travel is the class theme one week, constructing model rocket ships is more appropriate than painting self-portraits. Even open-ended activities to explore art materials and processes can be integrated with thematic units. For example, teachers can apply activities exploring cutting and gluing processes to a theme of one specific color by providing various materials and textures that are all the same color. In this way, teachers can connect a learning concept to experimentation with artistic processes.

Creating, Performing, and Responding

Three processes common to all branches of the arts—visual, musical, dance, dramatic, and performance art—are creating, performing, and responding. The first of these, creating, involves the genesis of the artistic product. There are several steps in creating. (1) Imagining is the step during which the artist develops his/her ideas and considers the concepts and feelings which s/he wants to communicate and express through the work. (2) Planning is the step during which the artist researches, experiments with, and designs the means by which s/he will present her/his ideas and emotions (e.g., the materials that will be used and how they will be manipulated to produce the desired effects). (3) Making, evaluating, and refining is the step during which the artist applies her/his skills and various techniques to create an artistic product that will bring her/his ideas and feelings to life. (4) Presenting is the step during which the artist exhibits visual art in a gallery, private exhibit, or another type of showing. The artist might also perform music, dance, theater, or performance art for an audience so that others can participate in and respond to the artwork.

Fundamental Artistic Processes Common to All Branches of the Arts

Works of art, whether visual, musical, dramatic, literary, dance, or performance art, all involve three basic and interrelated processes: creation of the work, performance of the work for others, and the response of others (e.g., audiences, participants, viewers, or readers). The artistic process of responding to artwork includes four steps. (1) Selection is the step during which the person(s) who will receive the artwork choose what they want to experience (possible choices include attending a gallery exhibit of paintings, drawings, or sculptures; going to see a theatrical play or a movie; attending a dance performance; attending/participating in a performance art show; or reading a book of poetry or prose). (2) Analysis is the step during which the viewers/audience/participants/readers see/hear and understand the components of the work, and mentally bring these components together to perceive the work as a whole. (3) Interpretation is the step during which those experiencing the work and/or its performance construct meaning from what they have witnessed, developing a personal response to the creator(s)' and performer(s)' expressions of concepts and emotions. (4) Evaluation is the final step, during which the respondent(s) assess the quality of the artwork and of its performance.

Lines

In visual media, a line is the path of a moving point; the edge of a flat or two-dimensional shape; or the outline of a solid, three-dimensional object. Lines are longer than they are wide. The term measure refers to the width of a line. Lines can be straight, curved, wavy, angular, or zigzag. Lines can be horizontal (side to side), vertical (up and down), or diagonal (at an angle between vertical and horizontal). Lines can also be implied. In this case, they are not physically present, but the artist's arrangement of other elements suggests lines, which organize the picture and/or guide viewers' eyes. The movement a line follows/appears to show is called direction. Where and how a line is placed in a picture/design is called location. Lines define areas, and imply or create open or closed shapes like circles, rectangles, etc. Line combined with shape creates implied volume in paintings/drawings and actual volume in sculptures. Lines express various qualities by being jagged, loopy, bold, repetitive, etc., and evoke different emotional and mental viewer responses.

Processes Involved in the Production and Reception of Works of Art

In all branches of the arts, artists and their audiences (who may also be participants in the case of performance art) complete three basic artistic processes that are closely related: creation, performance, and response. The performance process includes five steps. (1) Selecting is the step during which the artist makes a choice about what to present. For example, musicians choose pieces to play. Dancers choose choreographic pieces to perform. Visual artists select which of their paintings, drawings, sculptures, mobiles/stabiles etc. to display. Theater producers, directors, and actors choose a play to perform. (2) Analyzing is the step during which the performer researches the background of the chosen work and analyzes its structure to understand it and its import. (3) Interpreting is the step during which the performer develops a personal idea about what the work should express or accomplish. (4) Rehearsing, evaluating, and refining is the step during which the performer applies her/his skills and techniques to develop a personal interpretation that will enable her/his performance to make the work come alive. The artist then evaluates the performance, and makes further refinements to subsequent presentations. (5) Presenting is the final step, during which the artist performs the work for others.

Facilitating Student Learning with Creating, Performing, and Responding

The artistic processes have many steps in common. This interrelatedness among the processes informs students' development of educated responses to artworks. For instance, when students learn the step of evaluating their own artworks, they learn to apply better critical approaches when interpreting the artworks created by others. They also use their experiences to direct their selection of works they want to witness and respond to in the future. When students learn how to evaluate and refine their own work, this facilitates their subsequent evaluation and selection of others' works to watch, to perform themselves, and/or to purchase. Teachers can promote this by encouraging students to transfer their learning from one artistic process to another. For example, teachers can introduce students to others' work while they are creating their own so they can transfer what they learn about the creation process to the responding process. When students are solving specific creative/artistic problems, teachers can expose them to other artists' solutions and encourage students to consider these solutions.

Shape, Form, and Value

Shape refers to two-dimensional areas created by connecting lines to outline the contours of objects depicted in art. Shapes can be positive or negative (i.e. defined not by their own outlines, but by the edges of surrounding shapes). Shapes may be biomorphic (i.e. shapes found in nature) or geometric. Variations in value, texture, or color can make shapes stand out in a piece. Form is the three-dimensional projection of shape. Form has dimension and volume. In paintings and drawings, form appears to have mass, while in sculptures it actually does have mass. The term "form" can also be used to describe an artwork's overall structure. Value refers to the appearance and range of lights and darks seen in a visual work of art. Regardless of color, value varies between black and white, with an indefinite range of various shades of gray between these two absolutes.

Texture and Space

Texture refers to how rough or smooth a surface appears and/or feels. Everyday materials have texture, as do works of art. An object or a work of art can look and/or feel spongy or glassy, wet or dry, soft or hard, etc. Texture can be real, as with sandpaper and other rough-textured materials used to create works of art. Or, it can be illusory, as when materials appear hard or soft, but are really not. Space is defined as the measurable distance between predetermined points. It can be shallow or limited, with a foreground and a background; or it can be deep or extended, with a middle ground as well as a foreground and a background. Two-dimensional space has height and width; three-dimensional space has height and width, plus volume and time. Like negative shape (shape that is not defined by its own outlines, but by the surrounding shapes and their outlines), negative space appears in art. It is the space around and between the positive objects or shapes depicted. This negative space forms its own shapes around positive subjects.

Rhythm

In visual art, rhythm is achieved through repeating visual movement. Visual movement is created by arranging lines, shapes, and/or colors to give the viewer's eye a sense of motion and direction. Just as we hear rhythm in music through aural beats and varying note durations, we see rhythm in paintings through visual movement of lines, angles, shapes, and other elements. Just as Beethoven used repetition of musical phrases and themes to create mood, drama, and movement, artists use movement and repetition to create visual rhythm. For example, in "Nude Descending a Staircase, No. 2" (1912) by Marcel Duchamp, the artist depicts an abstracted human figure, repeating the figure using overlapping placements in a diagonal, downward pattern. The series of repeated shapes and angles gives the impression of viewing action in strobe lighting or via stop action photography. The figures are physically still, but visually convey the effect of moving down a staircase. By directionally repeating the figure, Duchamp shows movement and rhythm within the static medium of a painting.

Color

Color refers to the wavelengths of light reflected by a surface. Some wavelengths are absorbed by paints and other visual art media/materials; we do not see these. Other wavelengths are reflected; these are the ones we see as colors. Primary colors are pure, individual colors that cannot be separated into other colors or produced by mixing colors. The three primary colors are red, blue, and yellow. Secondary colors are combinations of two primary colors (e.g., orange = red + yellow, green = blue + yellow, and purple/violet = red + blue). Intermediate colors are produced by mixing a primary and a secondary color (e.g., red-orange, yellow-orange, blue-green, yellow-green, blue-violet, or red-violet). Colors are arranged on the color wheel. Analogous colors are adjacent to each other on the wheel. Examples of analogous colors include yellow and orange, orange and red, blue and green, and green and yellow. Complementary colors are opposite each other on the color wheel. Examples of complementary colors include blue and orange, yellow and purple, and red and green. Mixing equal parts of two complementary colors produces brown. Blue and predominantly blue colors are cool. Red, yellow, and predominantly red/yellow colors are warm. Colors identify objects, evoke moods, and influence emotions.

Rhythm

In visual art, rhythm is achieved through repeating visual movement. Visual movement is created by arranging lines, shapes, and/or colors to give the viewer's eye a sense of motion and direction. Just as we hear rhythm in music through aural beats and varying note durations, we see rhythm in paintings through visual movement of lines, angles, shapes, and other elements. Just as Beethoven used repetition of musical phrases and themes to create mood, drama, and movement, artists use movement and repetition to create visual rhythm. For example, in "Nude Descending a Staircase, No. 2" (1912) by Marcel Duchamp, the artist depicts an abstracted human figure, repeating the figure using overlapping placements in a diagonal, downward pattern. The series of repeated shapes and angles gives the impression of viewing action in strobe lighting or via stop action photography. The figures are physically still, but visually convey the effect of moving down a staircase. By directionally repeating the figure, Duchamp shows movement and rhythm within the static medium of a painting.

Balance

Balance refers to how visual weight is distributed in a work of visual art. In two-dimensional art like paintings, balance is the visual equilibrium among the painting's elements, which make the entire picture look balanced. Balance can be symmetrical (both sides are equal) or asymmetrical, with shapes and spaces that are unequal and/or unevenly distributed. This produces psychological rather than physical balance, creating tension and suggesting movement. Radial balance/symmetry uses images radiating from a center, such as wheel spokes or ripples around a pebble thrown into water. An example of balance is seen in the painting "Dressing for the Carnival" (1877) by Winslow Homer. The central figure of a carnival performer putting on his costume is the focal point. The performer is surrounded by two adult assistants and a group of fascinated children who are watching him. The shapes, values, and colors are balanced to produce overall visual equilibrium and unity (another organizing principle of art).

Visual Movement

Artists create a visual sense of movement in paintings to direct the viewer's eyes. Direction is frequently toward a focal point or area within the painting. Artists can direct movement along lines, edges, shapes, and colors, but especially along parts with equal value (dark/light), which best facilitates the eyes' movement. For example, in "Liberation of the Peon" (1931), Diego Rivera depicts soldiers liberating a slave by cutting the ropes binding him while clothing his nakedness with a blanket or garment. Paths of movement in the painting all lead to the focal point of the knife cutting the ropes. (Emphasis, another art/design principle, is also seen in how the action of freeing the peon is made more important than the soldiers performing that action.) By painting all humans in the scene with their eyes focused on the slave, Rivera creates movement directing our view toward him. At the same time, he painted all horses with their eyes focused out at the viewer, drawing the viewer into the scene.

Using Emphasis

Artists use the design principle of emphasis to call attention to particular elements in their works. Emphasis directs the viewer's focus to certain parts of a painting, and makes certain components of a work dominant. Emphasis can be achieved in art by emphasizing various design elements like value (light/dark), color, shape, line, etc. Artists also use contrast (e.g., contrasting values, colors, shapes, etc.) to create emphasis. To emphasize a focal area, a center of interest which focuses on the most important part of a painting, an artist can create visual emphasis through extreme contrasts of light and dark values. Strongly contrasting shapes and/or marked contrasts in other design elements also create visual emphasis. As an example of visual emphasis, in the painting "At the Moulin Rouge" (1892/1895), Henri de Toulouse-Lautrec emphasizes the focal area of a group of friends conversing in a cabaret through contrasting colors and values, as well as through movement directing the eye toward the group. His use of color, light, and shape also help create the scene's atmosphere.

Unity

One of the most important characteristics of a well-developed work of visual art is its visual unity. When we view a painting without unity, we may see a collection of disconnected parts that do not come together to form a whole. We may perceive it as fragmentary, disorganized, and incomplete. When an artist achieves visual unity, all of the elements in a painting appear to belong together. Unity affords paintings the quality of cohesion that makes them look and feel finished and complete. For example, in the painting "Starry Night" (1889), Vincent Van Gogh used his characteristic large, visible brush strokes in a swirly pattern throughout the landscape, providing visual unity through the texture, rhythm, pattern, and movement of the lines and shapes. He used predominantly cool colors (blues and bluish browns), providing unity through color. (He also provided emphasis by adding contrasting yellow stars.) The result is a unified painting whose elements work together, strongly conveying the atmosphere, mood, emotion, and story that the artist wanted to express.

Contrast

Contrast refers to significant differences in the values (lights and darks), colors, textures, shapes, lines, and other elements of visual artworks. Visual contrast creates interest and excitement, and avoids monotony in art. For example, in the painting "Still Life with Apples and Peaches" (1905), Paul Cézanne combined all seven elements and all seven principles of design to create a unified composition. Among these, he used at least eight kinds of contrast: (1) unpatterned vs. intricately patterned surfaces (pattern contrast); (2) soft vs. hard/found edges (edge contrast); (3) dark vs. light vs. middle values (value contrast); (4) pure vs. muted/blended colors (intensity contrast); (5) cool vs. warm colors (temperature contrast); (6) textured vs. smooth surfaces (texture contrast); (7) organic vs. geometric shapes (shape contrast); and (8) large vs. small objects/shapes (size contrast).

Pattern

Pattern is the organized or random repetition of elements. Music is made up of sound patterns. Visual patterns often appear in nature. Artists frequently create works featuring repeated designs that produce patterns inspired by those seen in the natural world. Visual art is enhanced by pattern, which enriches surface interest to augment visual excitement. For example, in "Numbers in Color" (1958-59), the artist Jasper Johns created a regular pattern by assembling 11 rows of 11 stacked rectangles each. He painted various numerical digits from 0 to 9 within most of the rectangles. He made these numbers look irregular by irregularly distributing, varying, and applying the colors he used. Many patterned paintings do not include a focal point or area. This often makes them look more like designs—even when they include recognizable images—than portraits, landscapes, still-lifes, or other types of paintings that do not have such repetitive patterning.

Pitch, Tempo, and Rhythm in the Musical Arts

Pitch is the frequency of a sound, such as a musical note. We hear high/middle/low frequency sound waves as high/middle/low pitched sounds. Various pitches are combined in musical compositions to create variety. A series of connected notes of different pitches creates a melody. Sounding (playing/singing) several pitches simultaneously and combining them produces harmonies and chords. Connected series of harmonies/chords in turn create harmonic/chord progressions. Tempo is the speed of music. Fast tempo can evoke happiness, excitement, fear, anger, or urgency. Slow tempo can evoke serenity, grandeur, solemnity, sadness, or ominousness. Musical compositions commonly direct the tempo using terms like andante (walking speed), adagio (slow), allegro (happy/quick), lento (slow), largo (expansively slow), etc. Rhythm includes the overall beat/time signature (number of beats per measure) and the variations among note lengths that produce patterns (e.g., legato describes smoothly connected series of notes, while staccato describes sharply disconnected notes that are cut short and sounded separately). Composers combine pitch, tempo, and rhythm in music to create atmosphere and mood, and to evoke emotion in listeners. They also arrange these elements to construct/recall musical themes/motifs within compositions.

Professional Relationships and Responsibilities

IDEA Law

Public Law 94-142, the Education for All Handicapped Children Act/Education for the Handicapped Act (EHA), passed in 1975; and Public Law 99-457, the EHA Amendments, passed in 1986, provided foundations that were expanded by new 1990 legislation. As a result, EHA was renamed the Individuals with Disabilities Education Act (IDEA). The IDEA's six main principles follow:

1. Publicly funded education cannot exclude any student because of the student's disability.
2. The rights of students with disabilities and of their parents are assured by the protection of due process procedures.
3. The parents of students with disabilities are encouraged to participate in their children's educations.
4. The assessment of all students must be fair and unbiased.
5. All students must be given a free, appropriate public education (FAPE), and it must be provided in the least restrictive environment (LRE) where the student and other students can learn and succeed.
6. Information related to students with disabilities and their families must be kept confidential.

Section 504, EHA, EHA Amendments, and ADA

In 1973, Section 504 of the Rehabilitation Act, also called Public Law 93-112, was enacted to ensure individuals with disabilities equal access to federally financed programs and to promote their participation in them. A child must have a physical or mental impairment that substantially limits a major life activity to be eligible for a free, appropriate public education (FAPE) under Section 504. This law stimulated motivation to educate students with disabilities, contributing to the passage of the Education for All Handicapped Children Act, also called Public Law 94-142, in 1975. This law provides that all children with disabilities must receive a FAPE provided in the least restrictive environment possible and individualized. Its procedural safeguards mandate due process. The 1986's EHA amendments, or Public Law 99-457 extended special education to disabled preschoolers aged 3 to 5 years; services to infants and toddlers are at each U.S. state's discretion. And 1990's Americans with Disabilities Act (ADA) requires access for disabled people to public buildings and facilities, transportation, and communication but does not cover educational services.

U.S. Federal Legislation Passed in 1997, 2001, and 2004

The 1990 Individuals with Disabilities Education Act (IDEA) was reauthorized in 1997 and numbered Public Law 108-446. It provided more access for children with disabilities to the general education curriculum and extended collaborative opportunities for teachers, other professionals, and families of children with disabilities. No Child Left Behind (NCLB, 2001, now the Every Student Succeeds Act, ESSA 2015), the reauthorization of the Elementary and Secondary Education Act (ESEA), stressed accountability for outcomes by identifying schools and districts needing improvement and assuring teacher quality. It required school performance data to include disabled students' standardized test scores. NCLB emphasized giving teachers and administrators better research information and schools more resources, parents more information about their children's progress and the school's performance, and more local flexibility and control in utilizing federal education funds and in improving teacher qualifications, for example, through alternative certifications. And, 2004's IDEA reauthorization, Individuals with Disabilities Education

Improvement Act (IDEIA), covers better alignment of NCLB with IDEA, appropriately identifying students needing special education, ensuring reasonable discipline while protecting special needs students defining highly qualified teachers, reducing paperwork, and increasing cooperation to decrease litigation.

Recent Legal Changes to the Americans with Disabilities Act

The ADA Amendments Act (ADAAA, 2009) overrules prior Supreme Court decisions narrowly interpreting the ADA. This qualifies many more conditions as disabilities.

- Physical or mental impairments substantially limiting one or more life activities now include immune system functioning; normal cell growth; brain, and neurological, respiratory, circulatory, endocrine, reproductive, digestive, bowel, and bladder functions, added to the existing activities of eating, sleeping, thinking, communicating, concentrating, lifting, and bending.
- Impairments include physical (deaf, blind, or wheelchair-bound); conditions (AIDS, diabetes, or epilepsy); mental illnesses and ADHD; record of impairment, for example, cancer in remission and regarded as impaired.
- Reasonable accommodations mean adaptations or modifications enabling persons with disabilities to have equal opportunities. The ADA describes this regarding equal employment opportunities, but it could also be interpreted relative to equal educational opportunities.
- Reasonable accommodations that would cause undue hardship, for example, financial, are not required.

Legal Responsibilities of EC Professionals

Historically, special education was introduced with the purpose of separating special-needs children from their normally developing peers. However, since 1991, the IDEA legislation has established the necessity of inclusion in normal care and educational environments, including EC settings, for children with disabilities. EC professionals know excluding any child is illegal. Another example of legal responsibilities is the "mandated reporter" status of caregivers/teachers/other adults working with children and families. They are legally required to report suspected child abuse and neglect; the law penalizes them for not reporting. For example, an EC teacher sees injuries to a child. S/he knows the mother has a new boyfriend, displays a fearful attitude, and responds evasively to teacher questions. Later, the child tells the teacher the boyfriend hurt him/her. The teacher pities the mother, realizing she needs the boyfriend financially and emotionally, and reporting suspected abuse could make the mother lose her children or their home. Regardless, the teacher must report suspicions by law, which was enacted for stopping violence against children.

Attributes Indicating EC Educators' Professionalism and Professional Responsibility

While care and instruction of young children are delivered through a variety of program types, EC educators share common general goals. They appreciate EC as a unique period in life. They work to educate holistically, considering the mind, feelings, and body of the whole child. The educational goals they develop are designed to support each child's fulfilling his/her individual potential within relationship contexts. EC professionals realize children are inseparable from their social milieus of family, society, and culture; they work to relate to and understand children in these contexts, while also appreciating and supporting family ties. They apply their knowledge of child development, teaching according to how children learn and what they need, and apply research in the field to differentiating common assumptions and myths from valid scientific findings. They have appropriate behavioral expectations for children at each developmental stage. EC professionals realize the significance of confidentiality: they never gossip or tell families personal information about other families. Lifelong learners, they set their own professional goals, pursuing ongoing professional development.

Interactions with Adults in the Learning Environment

Regarding teachers' roles, much of the focus is on observing children and their behaviors, helping children manage peer interactions, and giving children opportunities for developing peer-group social skills. Too often a similar emphasis is not accorded to teachers' reflecting on their interactions and behaviors with other adults; learning to collaborate with other adults; and developing skills for conflict resolution and managing disagreements with other adults. Some experts say teachers should work diligently and deliberately to make adult interactions integral parts of daily classroom activity. For group ECE settings to attain their goals, adults must make and implement plans collaboratively. However, mandatory staff meetings are commonly occupied with curricular and administrative requirements; beyond these, little or no attention or time is applied to nurturing adult-adult relationships. Adults interact during in-service trainings and professional development experiences, but outside of daily classroom settings. Nevertheless, these experiences can be used as foundations for better adult-adult communication within ECE contexts. Conscious efforts to develop adult-adult relationships benefiting children's growth, development, and learning are necessary.

Conditions Enabling and Supporting Positive Interactions Among Adults Within the ECE Setting

Adults engage in positive interactions with each other within ECE programs when they make time to share their anecdotal records and observations of their young students, and collaboratively plan instruction based on their collective contributions. When adults share information and communicate with one another about the children and their families with whom they work, they interact positively together. When EC educators engage in problem-solving activities and dialogues, these help them identify which learning goals and experiences they can make more effective for the children and how they can do this. Adults within ECE settings should engage in reciprocal exchanging of ideas about the EC learning environment and about how to share responsibilities for performing instructional tasks, rearranging classrooms as needed, setting up class projects, taking care of class pets and plants, and other such daily duties.

Adult-Adult Interactions Not Addressed in Research, Theoretical Literature, and Professional Development

ECE research contains little work addressing adults' cooperation and collaborative expertise with each other and the influences of these on children. However, the High/Scope curriculum model, The Creative Curriculum, and similar curriculum models and approaches do address adult-adult interactions by stressing how important teamwork is in planning lessons and sharing responsibilities and information. In addition, some educational experts have written about power struggles and other interactional dynamics in adult-adult relationships that can impede employee performance in a variety of settings. Professional development and training programs rarely include adult conflict-resolution techniques, instruction in working collaboratively, or adult learning principles. Hence educators must consider how their adult-adult interactions can support children's development of competence, capability, and confidence. Sharing instructional goals, planning learning experiences that support goals, and sharing responsibilities as a team for implementing projects establishes climates of safety and trust for children.

Applying Quality Time to EC Educators' Interactions with Adults

Educators have noted that attitudes and things we commonly say to children, e.g. "Your actions speak louder than your words" would equally benefit us addressing our own behaviors as adults. Applying the same principles we teach children to interactions among adults in the learning community can positively influence those interactions, which in turn affects adult-child/teacher-student interactions and overall classroom atmospheres. Without such atmospheres conducive to trust and honesty in adult relationships, educators can fall prey to misunderstandings and internalizing negative attitudes, which influence not only coworker interactions but moreover classroom climates. One solution is for adults in ECE to establish occasions affording "quality adult time." Psychotherapist and psychological theorist Virginia Satir, pioneer of family therapy, found interpersonal dynamics influenced by positive adult-adult communication. Trust-building, mutual colleague support, and sharing experiences/feelings—related or unrelated to classrooms—promote adult relationships that benefit teacher-learner relationships and thus enhance young children's development and learning.

Regulations Regarding the Confidentiality of Records

In EC settings, records kept about children and their families must be treated with strict confidentiality. EC centers/programs/preschools/agencies should limit access to student records to children's immediate family members; only those employees authorized; and agencies having legal authority to access records. Confidentiality of records and restricted access to them in all centers/programs/preschools/agencies that receive federal funding are mandated by the Family Educational Rights and Privacy Act (FERPA). Moreover, with the ongoing trend toward educational inclusion, many EC settings serve children with disabilities, whose student records are additionally subject to regulations under the federal Individuals with Disabilities Education Act (IDEA), and also to the special education laws of their respective U.S. states. An exception to the laws regarding records confidentiality is mandated reporting by EC personnel of suspected child abuse and neglect. Laws applying to child abuse and neglect supersede FERPA regulations. Legally, EC employees are both required to report suspected abuse and neglect of children, and immune from liability for releasing child records information relevant to their reporting.

Quality Care and Economic Considerations

To furnish and sustain quality care in EC settings is always challenging to care providers. It is even more so during difficult economic times. Many EC centers must face decisions whether to downsize the services they offer or to go out of business. When administrators choose to remain in operation, they encounter equally difficult decisions regarding how to reduce services, but not at the expense of quality. A legal issue related to such economic considerations is that EC personnel are often placed at legal risk when service quality is compromised. While EC employers, employees, young children's parents, and educational researchers are all interested in and pursue a definition of quality care, no single operational definition has been attained. However, EC professionals with ample work experience in EC centers have contributed various definitions. The consensus of their contributions includes the following common elements: a nurturing environment; employees trained in EC development and methods; age-appropriate curricula; sufficient space, equipment, and materials; safety and good maintenance of physical environments; and good parent-teacher communication.

Medical Care and Treatment Emphasized in Legal Regulations

The child care licensing regulations of each U.S. state government mostly govern children's medical care and treatment in EC settings. Overall, state regulations emphasize four areas of medical care and treatment: (1) Health requirements for all employees, such as having no communicable diseases; passing a TB test; having no health conditions preventing active child care; and maintaining accurate employee as well as child health records; (2) Administration by staff of medication to children being served in EC settings; (3) Management by EC staff of emergencies due to illness, injury, and accidents; and (4) Treatment of nonemergency minor illnesses, injuries, and accidents occurring to children in EC settings. To protect children's health and safety, EC programs/schools/centers must maintain written policies and procedures for emergency and nonemergency care. To protect personnel from litigation, they must adhere scrupulously to written policies and procedures. Litigation for damages/injury is likely when not following procedures. Not reporting suspected/observed child abuse/neglect and not completing accident reports also invite lawsuits.

Administration of Medication Guidelines

The administration of medication to children in EC settings has been subject to much controversy due to obvious issues of dangers and liability. EC centers/programs must write their policies and procedures to include their state government's licensing requirements for medical care and treatment, which they must follow closely. Experts recommend that parent and doctor permission be required for administering any prescription and nonprescription medications to children. EC settings should keep on file written parental consent for each medication, and review these records regularly for changes. They should also post separate charts, easily accessible to staff, with each child's name, medication, dosage, administration time, and teacher initials. These provide documentation of teachers following parent directions and can prevent mistakes. Staff should label all medications with the drug name, child's name, doctor's name and contact information, and administration instructions. EC centers seasonally and frequently contain many children simultaneously recovering from a variety of illnesses; labeling prevents giving children the wrong medication. Empty drug containers should be returned to parents.

Transportation from EC Locations and Emergency Medical Treatment by EC Employees

For a child's non-life-threatening medical emergencies, EC personnel should request transportation by the child's parents. However, if parents cannot transport the child, or in a more severe emergency, EC administrators should call an ambulance. In life-threatening emergencies that preclude waiting for an ambulance, EC administrators must designate the vehicle and responsible employee for transporting the child to the hospital; this information should be posted in the facility's emergency procedures. Administrators should keep the number of staff involved in emergency medical treatment to a minimum. Those employees they designate for involvement should be willing to take on the responsibility and should have current first aid training. The administrators can include a clause in these employees' job descriptions providing for their transporting children in the event of an emergency. The EC facility may also pay for additional or separate liability insurance coverage of the employees they designate as responsible for providing necessary emergency medical treatment.

Child Custody Issues Involving EC Facilities

EC facilities are affected by two types of issues involving child custody: (1) Parents are pursuing legal and/or physical custody of the child but they are not living together; and (2) State authorities have removed a child from the parents' legal and physical custody. Parents frequently demand the right to visit with and/or take the child home on occasion. Two types of custody are: legal custody, defined as an individual's or agency's right to make decisions on a child's behalf regarding the child's place of residence, medical treatment, and education; and physical custody, defined as an individual's or agency's right and responsibility to provide a child with immediate care, and a household or care facility for the present and immediate future. Physical custody does not include all of the rights of full legal custody. It is serious for a child to be in the middle of a custody battle between divorcing parents or between parents and foster parents; therefore EC facilities need the most concise, clear-cut guidelines possible.

Emergency Medical Treatment and First Aid Recommendations

EC programs and preschools must write specific, detailed procedures regarding emergency treatment and keep these on file. Children's parents, EC administrators, and EC staff need to be informed regarding what will occur in the event of a child's serious illness or injury. EC settings must also keep written, signed parental consent forms on file, as well as parent contact information, parental physician and hospital preferences, and health insurance information. EC staff should have current, regularly updated first aid training. First aid equipment should be stored in locations accessible to personnel, who should be frequently reminded of these locations. Lists of each staff member's first aid responsibilities and training should be posted, also accessibly. Licensing regulations require EC facilities to notify parents of emergencies; not doing so is subject to legal action. In non-life-threatening emergencies, staff should ask parents to furnish transportation and medical treatment. For grave emergencies, parental consent forms should be filed and updated semi-annually, including physician and hospital names, ambulance service, and other transportation procedures.

Non-Emergency Medical Illnesses

EC programs must keep procedures for, and reports on, non-emergency medical treatment of children on file just as they do for emergency procedures and reporting. Staff must contact and notify a sick child's parents, who decide if the child should leave the center/preschool. If so, parents should transport their child. Parental consent forms should authorize a doctor or nurse to provide routine medical treatment. EC centers/preschools should have sick children wait to be picked up in a location that is separate from other children and activities, but closely supervised by staff. For children with allergies, diabetes, and other chronic medical conditions, EC centers/preschools should not only keep this information on file in records, but also post it accessibly at all times for staff reference. Instructions for any special treatment should be included. For any health impairment(s) a child has that could potentially involve emergency treatment, directions for staff should be visibly posted, including specific employees designated to administer treatment. This protects children from harm and caregivers/educators from legal liability.

Custody Status

It is recommended that during a child's enrollment, EC programs procure a signed, dated document clarifying the child's custody status, including names, contact information, and relationships of all individuals authorized to pick up the child. Copies of any separation agreement/court decree should also be filed. Any time EC staff do not recognize an individual coming to pick up a child, they should ask the person to produce photo identification, which they should closely inspect. EC program administrators cannot make decisions regarding who has legal or physical custody of a child they serve. When a parent or other adult enrolls a child in an EC program, that adult is asked to list other persons to be contacted in the event of an emergency. EC administrators are advised to present all parents/guardians with a statement that the EC center will only release their child to someone the enrolling parent/adult listed on the emergency form as authorized to pick up the child.

Picking Up Children

Non-Custodial or Non-Authorized Adults Attempting to Pick Up Children

EC centers should always have up-to-date documentation on file of a child's custodial arrangements, signed and dated by the enrolling adult. If an adult not authorized to pick up the child attempts to do so, an EC administrator should inform that adult of the center's policies and procedures regarding custody. They may even show the unauthorized adult their copy of the custodial court order if needed. If the unauthorized adult then departs, the administrator must notify the enrolling adult of the incident; file a written report of it; meet with the custodial adult to clarify custody arrangements anew; document this meeting, including its date and signatures; and file the document in the child's record. If the unauthorized adult refuses to leave and makes a scene or threatens/displays violence, the EC administrator should call the police if needed. The EC center's having a procedure in place for protecting children against emotionally upsetting scenes and/or violent adult behavior is crucial to the children's safety and well-being.

Legal Responsibilities When Children Are Not Picked Up Timely

If a child is not picked up on time from an EC center at the end of its defined day, the EC center has the legal responsibility for the child's welfare as long as the child is on the premises. In the event that a child is left at the EC center for a long time and the parent/authorized adult has not notified the center why and/or when the child will be picked up, EC personnel are advised that keeping the child at the center is less likely to incur legal liability than for the child to stay at an EC staff member's home, for example. If the child has to be removed, it is important for EC staff to inform the police of this and where they are taking the child. If parents are chronically tardy picking up children, EC staff should review the child's information and/or inquire further of parents to ascertain reasons and possible solutions because they are legally responsible for reporting suspected child neglect.

Using Integrated Curricula

Integrating subject/domain content across the curriculum has been used for years at every educational level, from higher education to early childhood education. However, recent demands for accountability, as exemplified and escalated by No Child Left Behind, can distract educators from holistic and overall learning toward preoccupation with developing isolated skills and using test scores to measure achievement. But rather than discarding teaching methods proven effective, early childhood educators need to integrate newer, mandate-related practices into existing plans and methods. Teaching integrated curricula in early childhood classrooms has proven effective for both children and teachers. Integrating learning domains and subject content in turn integrates the child's developing skills with the whole child. When teachers use topics children find interesting and exciting, in-depth projects focusing on particular themes, and good children's literature, they give children motivation to learn the important concepts and skills they need for school and life success. Children should bring home from preschool not only further developed skills, but also knowledge useful and meaningful in life.

Using Manipulatives for Preschool Math Learning

Young children learn primarily through visually inspecting, touching, holding, and manipulating concrete objects. While they are less likely to understand abstract concepts presented abstractly, such concepts are likelier accessible to preschoolers through the medium of real things they can see, feel, and manipulate. Manipulatives are proven as effective learning devices; some early math curricula (e.g. Horizons) even require them. They are also particularly useful for children with tactile or visual learning styles. Many math manipulatives are available for sale, e.g. linking cubes; 3-dimensional geometric shapes and "geoboards"; large magnetized numbers for whiteboards; weights, scales, and balances for measurements; math blocks; math games; number boards and color tiles; flash cards; play money, toy cash registers, and activities; objects for sorting and patterning; or tangrams for recognizing shapes, reproducing and designing patterns, and spatial problem-solving. Teachers can create homemade math manipulatives using bottle caps/lids; seashells, pebbles/stones; buttons; keys; variously sized, shaped, and colored balls; coffee stirrers; or cardboard tubes from paper products.

Helping Young Children Use Inquiry and Discovery in Science

EC teachers are advised to "teach what they know," i.e. use materials with which they are familiar. For example, teachers who like plants can have young children plant beans, water and watch them grow, moreover incorporating this activity with the story "Jack and the Beanstalk." Teachers can bring in plants, leaves, and flowers for children to observe and measure their sizes, shapes, or textures. Experts recommend teachers utilize their everyday environments to procure learning materials, such as pine needles and cones; loose feathers and leaves found outdoors; animal fur from pets or groomers; and/or snakeskins or turtle shells from local pet stores. Experts advise teachers to use their observational skills during inquiry and discovery activities: if children apply nonstandard and/or unusual uses of some materials, teachers should observe what could be a new discovery, wherein students teach adults new learning, too. Teachers should let children play with and explore new materials to understand their purposes, uses, and care before using them in structured activities.

Benefits of Aesthetic Experiences

To help children learn color names and develop sensory discrimination and classification abilities, some art museums offer preschool lessons, which teachers can also use as models. For example, a teacher can read a children's story or sing a song about color, then present a painting/artwork for children to examine, and then a separate display with circles/squares/ovals of colors used by the artist, asking children to name these and any other colors they know, and identify any other colors the artist used not represented in the second display. The teacher then demonstrates how mixing produces other colors. After this demonstration with children's discussion, the teacher gives each child a piece of heavy-duty paper and a brush. The teacher pours about an inch-sized puddle of each of the three primary colors—red, blue, and yellow—in the middle of each child's paper. The teacher then tells the children to use their brushes to explore mixing colors and see the variety of other colors they can create.

Process Skills Developed by Preschool Science Programs

Experts find three process skills that good EC science programs help develop are observation, classification, and communication. Young children are inherently curious about the world and hence enjoy many activities involving inquiry and discovery. Teachers can uncover science in many existing preschool activities. For example, since young children relate to activities focusing on themselves, teachers can have them construct skeletons of dry pasta, using their pictures as heads. Cooking activities involve science, as do art activities. Teachers can have children explore various substances' solubility in water, which colors are produced by mixing which other colors, etc. They can have them compare/contrast similarities/differences among objects. They can create inexpensive science centers using animal puppets; models; thematically-related games, puzzles, books, and writing materials; mirrors, prisms, magnifiers; scales, magnets; and various observable, measurable objects. Teachers should regularly vary materials to sustain children's interest.

Preschool Activities for Developing Physical Coordination, Fine Motor Skills, and Large Muscle Skills

Preschoolers are more likely to fall because their lower bodies are not yet developed equally to their upper bodies, giving them higher centers of gravity. Therefore, seeing how long they can balance on one foot and hopping exercises help improve balance and coordination. Hopping races let preschoolers participate in groups and observe peer outcomes, which can also enhance self-confidence and supporting others. "Freeze dancing" (like Musical Chairs without the chair-sitting), without eliminations, provides physical activity and improves coordination. Using writing implements, tying shoes, and playing with small items develop fine motor skills. With preschoolers, it is more effective and developmentally appropriate to incorporate fine motor activities into playtime than to separate quiet activity from play. For example, on nature walks, teachers can have children collect pebbles and twigs and throw them into a stream, developing coordination and various muscles. Running, skipping, and playing tag develop large muscle skills. Kicking, throwing, and catching balls give good unstructured exercise without game rules preschoolers cannot understand. Preschoolers' short attention spans preclude long activity durations.

Benefits of the Line in Visual Arts

Activities focusing on line in art help young children expand their symbol recognition, develop their comparison-making ability, and facilitate shape recognition. Teachers can begin by singing a song or reading a children's story about lines. Then they can present one painting/drawing/artwork and help children point at various kinds of lines that the artist used. The teacher can draw various line types on a separate piece of paper, e.g. wavy, pointy, spiral, and ask children to find similar lines in the artwork. Then the teacher can ask children to try drawing these different lines themselves. Teachers should also inform children of various tools for drawing lines and let them experiment with these, e.g. crayons, pencils, markers, chalk, paint. An EC teacher can also supply butcher paper or other roll paper for each child to lie down on in whatever creative body positions they can make. The teacher outlines their body shapes with a marker. Then the teacher has the children explore drawing different kinds of lines, using various kinds of drawing tools, to enhance and personalize their individual body outlines.

Aesthetic Experiences Involving Shape

Giving young children learning activities that focus on shape used in art helps them develop their abilities to form concepts and identify discrepancies. Manipulating basic geometric shapes also stimulates their creative thinking skills and imaginations, as well as developing early geometric math skills. For example, an EC teacher can first read aloud a children's book about shapes, of which many are available. After reading it through, the teacher can go back through the story asking children to point to and name shapes they recognize. Then the teacher can show children an artwork. Using line drawings and/or solid geometric shapes, they discuss what shapes the artist used. The teacher can help children arrange solid shapes to form different images (people, flowers, houses). The teacher can then give children paper pulp trays/heavy paper/board, assorted wooden/cardboard/plastic shapes, and instructions to think and arrange shapes they can make with them, and then give them glue to affix the shapes to their trays/paper/board. They can paint their creations after the glue dries.

Providing Affective Learning Experiences

Providing affective experiences supports young children's emotional development, including understanding and expressing their emotions. These enable development of emotional self-regulation/self-control. Emotional development is also prerequisite to and supportive of social interactions and development. Affective activities also help teachers understand how children feel, which activities they find most fascinating, and/or why they are not participating. "Feelings and Faces" activities are useful. For example, a teacher can have each child draw four different "feeling" faces on paper plates—e.g. happy, sad, angry, confused, excited—and discuss each. A teacher can offer various scenarios, like learning a new song, painting a picture, getting a new pet, or feeling sick, and ask children how they feel about each. Then the teacher can give them new paper plates, having them draw faces showing feelings they often have. Gluing Popsicle sticks to the plates turns them into "masks." The teacher can prompt the children on later days to hold up their masks to illustrate how they feel on a given day and about specific activities/experiences.

Most Important Social Skills

Experts find it crucial for young children's later success in school and life to have experiences that develop understanding of their own and others' emotions; constructive management of their strong feelings; and skills in forming and maintaining relationships. Young children use earlier developed motor skills like pushing/shoving, biting, hitting, or kicking, to get what they want rather than later developing verbal skills. Since physical aggression is antisocial, social development includes learning more acceptable, verbal emotional expressions. "Punch and Judy"-type puppet-shows depicting aggression's failures entertain preschoolers; discussing puppet behavior develops social skills. Teachers have children say which puppets they liked/disliked and considered good/bad; what happened; what might happen next; and how puppets could act differently. Teachers can reinforce children's discussion of meeting needs using words, not violence. Many read-aloud stories explain why people behave certain ways in social contexts; discussion/question-and-answer groups promote empathy, understanding, and listening skills. Assigning collaborative projects, like scrapbooking in small groups, helps young children learn cooperation, turn taking, listening, and verbally expressing what they want.

Exploring Texture in Art

Preschoolers learn much through looking at and touching concrete materials. Activities involving visual and tactile examination and manipulation plus verbal discussion enhance young children's representational/symbolic thinking abilities. Such activities also enable children to explore various ways of representing different textures visually. Teachers can provide "feely bags/boxes"—bags/boxes with variously textured items inside, e.g. sandpaper, fleece, clay, wool, or tree bark—for children to feel and describe textures before seeing them, and identify objects based on feel. A teacher can then show children a selected artwork; they discuss together which textures are included, e.g. smooth, rough, jagged, bumpy, sharp, prickly, soft, or slippery. The teacher can then demonstrate using plaster/thickened paste/clay how to create various textures using assorted tools (e.g. tongue depressors, plastic tableware, chopsticks, small toys, or child-safe pottery tools) and have children experiment with discovering and producing as many different textures as they can. After children's products dry, they can paint them the next day.

Providing Affective Experiences and Promoting Emotional Development, Physical Activity, and Creativity

Early childhood teachers can help children understand their feelings and others' feelings, express their emotions, engage in physical exercise, use creative thinking, and have fun by using emotional movement activities. For example, the teacher can begin with prompting the children to demonstrate various types of body movements and postures, like crawling, walking, tiptoeing, skipping, hopping, crouching, slouching, limping, or dancing. Then the teacher can ask the children which feelings they associate with each type of movement and body position. The teacher can play some music for children to move to, and give them instructions such as "Move like you are happy....like you are sad....like you are scared....like you are surprised....like you are angry...." Teachers can also use "freeze"/"statue" dances or games, wherein children move to music and must freeze in position like statues when the music stops; for affective practice, teachers instruct children to depict a certain emotion each time they freeze in place.

Genetic and Biological Influences on Children Relative to Addictive Behaviors

Adopted children with one or both biological parents having histories of alcohol abuse, criminal records, and/or major psychiatric illness are at double the risk for drug abuse as those having biological parents without such histories. While this risk is genetic, differential environmental influences can exacerbate or mitigate children's biological risk for engaging in addictive behaviors. For example, adopted children who experience difficulties in their adopted families, such as deaths or divorce, are at higher risk of developing drug abuse problems. Conversely, children whose biological parents' histories put them at higher genetic risk for abusing drugs—but who were adopted into loving, stable families—are less at risk for developing addictions. Researchers conclude that children with higher genetic risks for addiction are more vulnerable to adverse environmental influences in their adopted families than children with lower genetic risks. Also, genetic risks become less powerful in adoptive families having lower environmental risk factors.

Alfred Adler's Theoretical Concepts of the Effects of Birth Order

Only Child and Oldest Child

Neo-Freudian psychologist Alfred Adler proposed that a child's birth order relative to other children in a family is associated with corresponding influences on the child's personality and behaviors. For example, Adler found that the only child is regarded as a miracle of birth by parents with no prior experience of having a baby. This child receives the undivided attention of both parents, who may be overprotective of the child and/or spoil him/her. Some general characteristics of only children include preferring adults' company, using adult language, enjoying being the center of attention from adults, and finding it difficult to share with other children. Adler said the oldest/older child has been "dethroned"/displaced by a younger sibling and must learn to share. Parents often have very high expectations of the oldest/older child, give him/her much responsibility, and expect him/her to set an example for younger siblings. Older/oldest children may turn to fathers once a sibling is born. They may feel entitled to power, developing strict/authoritarian attitudes/behaviors. Given encouragement, they can develop helpful attitudes/behaviors.

Second Child and Middle Child

Psychoanalyst and theorist Adler included birth order as one factor in his study of influences on personality development. He identified general tendencies associated with each family birth position. For example, the second-born child was described by Adler as having a "pacemaker" in that there is always an older sibling ahead of this child. Adler found that the results of this position include the child's becoming more competitive out of attempts to overtake the elder sibling. He noted that competition could devolve into sibling rivalry. A second child might develop into a rebellious sort or might develop a habit of always trying to "top" or exceed everybody else's accomplishments. Adler described the middle child in a family as being "sandwiched" between older and younger siblings, so that s/he can feel "squeezed out" of any privileged or significant position. Some middle children may grow up to fight against injustice or unfairness; others may encounter difficulty establishing places for themselves. Some middle children develop even-tempered dispositions, with no extreme opinions and "take-it-or-leave-it" attitudes.

"Ghost Child" and the Adopted Child

Adlerian psychoanalytic theory includes family birth order as an influence on personality development and behavior. For example, Adler described a child who is born after an older child has died as having a "ghost" ahead of him/her. Such a child, called a "ghost child," is likely to be subject to overprotection by the mother, who fears losing him/her after losing a child previously. The child may respond to parental overprotectiveness by taking advantage of the parent to get what s/he wants. Alternatively, some "ghost" children resent feeling parental comparisons to the deceased child, whose memory parents have idealized; in this case, the child may rebel. Adler said adoptive parents can be so grateful to have a child and so anxious to make up for the child's loss of biological parents, that they may spoil him/her; thus, the adopted child is more liable to develop very demanding, spoiled behaviors. The adopted child may ultimately either resent his/her biological parents for rejecting/leaving him/her or idealize them, negatively comparing the adoptive parents.

Youngest Child and Twin Children

In his psychoanalytic theory, Alfred Adler included birth order as one family influence on child personality development. For example, he found that the youngest child in a family, like an only child, is never "dethroned" or displaced by a new sibling. However, unlike an only child, the youngest sibling has many "parents" in the form of older siblings who help to raise, instruct, and influence him/her. Youngest siblings are often spoiled by the attentions of parents plus older siblings. Some youngest children continue to feel and behave like the "baby" of the family indefinitely. Many youngest children, always being littlest, wish to be bigger than siblings. As they grow, youngest siblings may make grandiose plans that never succeed. Adler found with twins, one is usually more active or stronger, and is often perceived by the parents as older—s/he may have been born a minute earlier and/or they perceive him/her as more mature. The stronger twin may develop as the leader; the other may develop problems with identity.

Familial Birth Order, Only Boy Among Girl Siblings, Only Girl Among Boy Siblings, Boy with All Boy Siblings, and Girl with All Girl Siblings

Adler found that the ways children are perceived and treated by parents and siblings relative to their birth order contribute to their personality formation and behavior. For example, Adler stated the only boy with girl siblings, surrounded by females when the father is not there, can develop either of opposite extremes: he may engage excessively in behaviors to prove he is the "man of the family" or develop effeminate behaviors through identifying with surrounding females. Adler found when a child is the only girl among male siblings, her older brothers can behave protectively toward her. An only girl among boys may make efforts to please the father and develop either of two opposing extremes: becoming a tomboy to compete with brothers or developing very feminine behaviors to differentiate from them. In families with all-male or all-female children, Adler noted parents who wanted a child of the other sex might dress one child as the opposite sex. The child may either exploit this role reassignment or strongly object to it.

Murray Bowen's Family Systems Theory

Dr. Bowen identified four basic family relationship patterns within what he called the Nuclear Family Emotional System. These patterns dictate where problems develop when the family system is under tension. Bowen labeled these patterns Marital Conflict; Dysfunction in One Spouse; Impairment of One or More Children; and Emotional Distance, which latter is associated with the first three. In Impairment of One or More Children, the parents focus their anxieties on one or more of their children. Their perception of the child(ren) is either negative or idealized. The more the parents focus on one child, the more that child reciprocally focuses on them, becoming more reactive to parental expectations, needs, and attitudes than siblings are. This process undermines the child's differentiation of self, a key factor in healthy individual development according to Bowen. The child becomes more susceptible to internalizing or externalizing family tensions, affecting his/her social relationships, school performance, and physical and mental health.

Family Projection Process

In the Family Projection Process, Dr. Murray Bowen found that parents can project their anxieties onto their children. When parents worry overly that something is wrong with one child, they may see everything the child does as proof of that worry. Their excessive efforts to remedy the child's "problem" can actually cause the child to develop the problem in reality, as the child's self-image becomes aligned with parental perceptions. While parents with such worries usually feel guilty of not giving the "problem" child enough attention, they have in fact directed more attention to this child than his/her siblings. Bowen found that children less engaged in this process have more realistic, mature relationships with parents and develop into more goal-oriented, less reactive, and less emotionally needy individuals. Both parents participate equally in the process in different ways; both are insecure relative to the child, but Bowen said typically one parent pretends to feel secure with the other's complicity.

In his theory, Bowen referred to the way parents transmit their emotional issues to children as the Family Projection Process, which involves three steps: (1) A parent focuses on a child, fearing something is wrong with that child. (2) The parent perceives the child's behavior as confirmation of this fear. (3) The parent then treats the child as though something really is wrong. When parents try to "fix" what they perceive is a problem in the child, their perception can become a self-fulfilling prophecy as the child eventually embodies that perception. For example, if parents perceive a child as helpless and are always helping her excessively, the child's self-image comes to mirror the parents' perception; the child becomes de facto helpless and dependent even though she may not have been so initially. The more intense this process is, the greater relationship sensitivities children develop, beyond those of their parents.

MEGA Practice Test

1. A teacher asks her students to compare and contrast two animals they saw at the zoo. This is an example of what level of Bloom's taxonomy?

   A. Knowledge
   B. Comprehension
   C. Application
   D. Analysis

2. Students studying fractions manipulate "fraction blocks," blocks cut to represent fractional parts, to learn the concept of adding and subtracting fractions. Which level of development as described by Piaget does this activity demonstrate?

   A. Sensory-motor stage
   B. Pre-operational stage
   C. Concrete operational stage
   D. Formal operations stage

3. According to Kohlberg, at which developmental level do children understand that good behavior is expected?

   A. Post-Conventional
   B. Conventional
   C. Pre-Conventional
   D. Adolescent

4. Erikson's stages of development include all of the following except

   A. Young childhood
   B. Middle adulthood
   C. Adolescence
   D. Late childhood

5. In Bronfenbrenner's organization of child development, the family or classroom is considered a

   A. Chronosystem
   B. Microsystem
   C. Macrosystem
   D. Mesosystem

6. One of Vygotsky's major contributions to the field of early childhood development is the concept of

   A. Punishment/obedience
   B. A taxonomy of learning skill levels
   C. The importance of play as a learning activity
   D. The formal operations stage of development

7. Which of the following is a component of the Constructivist learning theory?

   A. Students, teachers, and classmates establish knowledge cooperatively every day
   B. Students are taught to develop skills in problem solving and critical thinking
   C. Children only learn language and culture through interaction with adults and other children
   D. It is important to help the learner gain an understanding of how knowledge is constructed

8. Social and behavioral theories of learning stress the importance of

A. Good behavior on the part of students
B. The social interactions of students that aid or inhibit learning
C. A reward system for good behavior or growth in skills
D. The direct connection between thoughts and speech

9. A teacher becomes aware that a certain student's family is in a crisis situation. What is his or her best course of action?

A. Counsel the child on how best to handle the situation at home
B. Contact the parents with a direct offer to help with their problems
C. Report the crisis situation to school or civil authorities
D. Attempt to deal with the student as well as possible despite the situation

10. Which of the following is the best way to assist children from families with limited incomes?

A. Lower expectations for these children's achievements in the classroom
B. Cooperate with school administrators and public officials to provide such assistance as a free lunch program and/or some academic assistance
C. Counsel parents on ways to economize with their limited financial resources
D. Provide the best possible instruction without any need for intervention or public assistance

11. The teacher notices that a student's attention in the classroom is decreased. The student seems restless and unable to concentrate. Which of the following may be the cause of this change in behavior?

A. The child is coming down with an illness, such as the flu
B. A problem has developed at home, such as divorce or abuse
C. The child has entered a period of rapid physical growth which distracts him or her from cognitive activity
D. All or any of the above

12. Which of the following is a symptom of an emotionally-neglected child?

A. Extreme focus on school activities, seeking self-esteem
B. Acts of jealousy or aggression toward other children
C. Cooperative attitude in the classroom and on the playground
D. Initiating social interaction with other students in the class at inappropriate times

13. Which of the following is an important aspect of allowing and encouraging children's play?

A. Children need frequent opportunities to rest and relax
B. Play teaches children cooperation and sharing
C. Play encourages competition and opposition
D. Play time gives the teacher a much needed rest period

14. What personal benefits can a young child obtain from play?

A. Development of motor skills, such as hand-eye coordination
B. Development of personal interests
C. The ability to entertain himself or herself when alone
D. All of the above

15. Social development and cognitive development often progress together because

A. The more knowledge a child has, the more social he becomes
B. As children are developing physically, they lose interest in social interactions
C. Children develop the dexterity to show their cognitive development
D. All areas of development—physical, social, and cognitive—are interrelated

16. The concept of latent development is important for teachers because:

A. Teachers can be more patient with students if they understand their latency
B. Teachers can wait until a student demonstrates complete ability in a certain skill area
C. Teachers will be able to instruct the class as a whole group if they understand the stage at which everyone in the classroom is developing
D. Developing skills may give clues for the next stage of instruction a student will need

17. A flat or agitated expression coupled with incoherent speech is a major symptom of

A. Autism
B. Drug or alcohol abuse
C. Schizophrenia
D. Intellectual disabilities

18. Which of the following actions are important for a teacher to do to create learning conditions for students with disabilities?

A. Use a child-centered approach to instruction
B. Help students identify their own learning needs
C. Structure learning experiences appropriate to the needs of the disabled student
D. All of the above

19. When a child begins to act violently, breaking things and quarreling with other students, teachers should see this change in behavior as a

A. Sign of intellectual disabilities
B. Sign of emotional difficulties
C. Sign the child is becoming autistic
D. Sign the child is abusing drugs or alcohol

20. If a child exhibits loss in cognitive thinking, social behavior, and usual academic progress, the teacher should suspect that the child

A. May be developing schizophrenia
B. May be having emotional problems at home
C. May be epileptic
D. May be abusing drugs

21. What makes a child eligible for special education services?

A. Falling behind academically and refusing to do any work at school
B. Having a diagnosed physical or emotional disability that has been evaluated professionally
C. Recommendation by the classroom teacher that the child needs additional help
D. Request by parents for the child to be given special education services

22. If a child demonstrates a lack of concentration in the classroom and also becomes easily agitated, he or she may be suffering from

A. Lack of sleep and/or nutrition
B. Little verbal interaction at home
C. A significant mental or emotional disability
D. Severe physical abuse

23. At what age do children normally demonstrate a speech pattern that is at least 75% intelligible to strangers?

a. Two years
b. Three years
c. Four years
d. Five years

24. If a child appears delayed in speech development, which of the following is the best course to follow?

A. Take a wait-and-see approach, as there are wide variations in patterns of speech development
B. Use in-depth evaluations and early intervention to assist the child with language delays
C. Help the child with common developmental speech problems, such as saying "w" for "r"
D. Have the child repeat common words and phrases after an adult pronounces them

25. Which of the following is NOT a characteristic of a child with emotional disturbance?

A. Lower academic performance
B. Social skills deficits
C. Aggressive behaviors
D. Exaggerated efforts to make friends

26. How should the teacher best deal with an academically talented student who typically finishes work ahead of other students and tends to get into mischief while waiting for others to finish?

A. Reprimand the student and remind him or her that his talents require setting a good example.
B. Assign the student an appealing task related to the subject area that requires creativity, research, and/or in-depth study of the subject, such as creating a play or making a collage
C. Permit the early finisher to have additional play time or extended recess as a reward for rapid completion of assignments
D. Have the student tutor or help those who are not finished because they are having difficulty with the assignment

27. The most important factor for the teacher to keep in mind when teaching students with disabilities is

A. Vary instructional pace and content to meet the specific needs of disabled students
B. Slow the pace of classroom instruction to give the disabled students time to catch up
C. Group the disabled students into a special section set apart from the regular students
D. Insist that disabled students remain in their seats and focus on instruction

28. Seeking the appropriate method for meeting the needs of a disabled student is most often initiated by

A. Parents
B. A school's Child Study Team
C. Community agencies
D. The student's classroom teacher

29. Involvement of parents in developing a student's IEP (individualized education program) is essential because:

A. An IEP must be approved by a parent before it can be enacted
B. Parents know their children's needs, and an IEP must be tailored to those needs
C. Teachers do not have the legal rights to discuss student needs with community representatives
D. Students will not be willing to follow an IEP unless they have parental support

30. What is meant by the "least restrictive environment" policy of the IDEA?

A. It is permissible to retain disabled students without passing them to the next grade level
B. Students with disabilities need to be instructed in special classes
C. Students with disabilities must be educated in an environment appropriate to them and their non-disabled peers, often a regular classroom
D. Disabled students must be permitted to participate in the same classroom instruction as their non-disabled peers, even when it does not quite meet their needs

31. An IEP is a plan for

A. Providing a tutor for an educationally handicapped student
B. Providing counseling for an emotionally disturbed student
C. Assisting parents in their problems handling a disabled student
D. Assisting students in ways beyond what the classroom teacher can provide

32. A 504 differs from an IEP in that the 504

A. Focuses on helping emotionally or physically disabled students within the classroom
B. Is a legal document and requires formal assessment of the disability
C. Requires the student to be referred for help by a parent or family member
D. Requires regular monitoring and may be adjusted during the school year

33. Which of the following is NOT a reason for having a parent conference?

A. The teacher wants to share information about the child's behavior and progress with the parents
B. The teacher wants to receive information about the child from the parents
C. The teacher wants to ask for parent support or involvement in specific activities
D. The child's behavior is so difficult that the teacher wants the parents to withdraw the child from school

34. What is the advantage of placing students in community organizations like the ASB (Associated Student Body) or the PTSA (Parent Teacher Student Association)?

A. These organizations help students to become politically savvy and be able to manipulate the rules of their school
B. These organizations help students who are falling behind in school with tutoring and mentoring
C. These organizations provide opportunities for students to develop leadership skills and learn to appreciate the value of collaborative processes
D. Membership in these organizations can be listed on a student resume when the student is applying to colleges or universities

35. Which of the following genres is most important for children just beginning to become readers in grades K, 1, and 2?

A. Alphabet books, wordless picture books, and easy-to-read books
B. Legends and tall tales
C. Biographies and informational books
D. Chapter books and fantasy books

36. Which of the following is NOT a goal of children's literature?

A. Focus on choices, morals, and values
B. Instruct students through entertaining stories
C. Promote an interest in reading itself
D. Instruct students in the sciences, such as mathematics and biology

37. In which genre does the literature rely on the reader's suspension of disbelief about magical and mythical creatures?

A. Science fiction
B. Fantasy
C. Action and adventure
D. Historical fiction

38. A story about a young detective who solves mysteries using mental and physical skills would be classified as

A. Action and adventure
B. Historical fiction
C. Horror and ghost stories
D. Biography

39. The statement, "He ran away like a startled rabbit," is an example of

A. Simile
B. Metaphor
C. Symbolism
D. Repetition

40. Young children are more likely to respond to analogies in stories than to metaphors because

A. They are old enough to understand the abstract thinking and symbolism that analogies express

B. The ability to understand the kinds of abstraction expressed in metaphors is not developed until later in childhood

C. They can apply the concepts expressed in analogies to their own daily lives, but metaphors do not compare things that children are familiar with

D. Metaphors and symbols are usually found only in books that children find boring because of their abstractions

41. When students compare nonfiction literature to fictional literature, what differences will they find?

A. Nonfiction stories will be told in logical order and will relate only the facts, while fictional stories are never told in logical order

B. Fictional stories deal with plot, characters, setting, and themes, and nonfiction does not

C. In addition to plot, character, setting, and theme, a nonfiction work will also introduce interpretations, theory, and research

D. Students will find few, if any, differences between these two types of literature because they are essentially the same

42. Which of the following would you expect children in grades k–2 to learn by being exposed to both fictional and nonfictional literature?

A. How to tell fiction from nonfiction

B. How to do research to find information

C. How to tell if a nonfiction writer is writing from a biased viewpoint

D. How to understand themes, theories, and settings

43. In selecting literature for children, the most important first step a teacher should perform is to evaluate

A. Whether the characters are interesting

B. Whether the plots are appealing

C. Class composition and preferences

D. The reading level of the material

44. What is the best way for a teacher to make sure that books in the classroom are at an appropriate reading level, neither too easy nor so difficult that beginning readers will become frustrated?

A. Administer a reading pretest to the class before selecting suitable books

B. Purchase books that are easy enough for even the most beginning of readers

C. Make sure that all the books are just slightly above students' reading level, so they will grow

D. Provide a wide variety of reading materials for children to choose from

45. One of the most important elements in children's literature that captures children's interest is

A. Character

B. Accuracy

C. Information

D. Vocabulary

46. If a teacher does not have time to pre-read all the books she selects for her classroom, what is a good alternative?

A. Look at children's book reviews in professional materials
B. Seek input from children themselves about their favorite books
C. Seek the assistance of the school librarian
D. All of the above

47. The adaptation of language in a piece of writing to meet the author's purpose or audience is called

A. Theme
B. Point of view
C. Style
D. Voice

48. The perspective from which a story is told is called

A. Theme
B. Point of view
C. Style
D. Voice

49. In Mr. Booker's first grade classroom, students are studying marine animals in science. Mr. Booker wants to select a book to read to the class that will enhance their understanding of this subject while at the same time capturing their interest in a story. Which of the following would be the best choice?

A. *The Wild Whale Watch*, part of the Magic School bus series, a chapter book about whales
B. *The Whale Watchers Guide*, a book designed to help plan a whale-watching trip
C. M*oby Dick,* a famous 19th century novel about a man and a white whale
D. *The Pacific Ocean*, a book describing the ocean floor, tides, wave formation, and currents

50. Which of the following describes one difference between role-play writing and early writing?

A. In role-play writing, the child writes in scribbles that are only meaningful to him or her. In early writing, the child uses real letters
B. In early writing, the child writes in scribbles that are only meaningful to him or her. In role-play writing, the child writes in groups of words with a period at the end
C. In role-play writing, the child writes in simple forms of language, usually the way the word sounds. In early writing, the child starts to use sight words and familiar text
D. In early writing, the child has a sense of audience and a purpose for writing. In role-play writing, the child writes from the point of view of an imaginary character

51. Which of the following is a developmental skill a child should have before beginning to write?

A. Large muscle control
B. Ability to speak coherently
C. Small muscle control
D. Ability to hold a pencil correctly

52. A child using the prewriting strategy called "free writing" will

A. Make a list of all ideas connected with the chosen topic
B. Create a visual map on paper to connect ideas
C. Ask the questions "Who?," "What?," "When?," and "Where?"
D. Write thoughts and ideas without stopping to edit them

53. Which of the following is NOT a prewriting strategy?

A. Brainstorming
B. Visual mapping of ideas
C. Asking questions
D. Organizing writing into paragraphs

54. In the organization stage of writing, the writer

A. Determines the purpose, thesis, and supporting details of the written work
B. Brainstorms ideas for items to include in the written work
C. Submits the writing to a classmate for editing
D. Writes the introduction and conclusion

55. Maria's topic sentence is "My family prepares for holidays in a big way." Which of the following would be the best supporting detail to follow that sentence?

A. Holidays are just a waste of everyone's time and money
B. First, we decide who is going to host the holiday dinner
C. In my family are me, my brother, my sister, and our parents
D. Afterwards we all help clean up and then relax

56. Which of the following is true of the introduction to a written piece?

A. It should be written first
B. It should be written last
C. It should reinforce the points made in the piece
D. It is the least important part of a piece of writing

57. Which of the following is not a method of peer editing?

A. Pairs of students analyze each others' sentences for variety
B. Groups of students ask questions of the author to make the writing more clear
C. Students work together to perform a final edit
D. Students decide whether another student's essay is good writing or poor writing

58. Which of the following should not be capitalized?

A. State names
B. Small words like "of" in titles
C. Proper names
D. Main words in titles of written work

59. Elena wrote the following paragraph:

> I believe that everyone should try to care for our planet. The best ways to do this are through recycling and using natural energy instead of fossil fuels. The supply of fossil fuels such as oil and coal will be used up some day, so we should try now to use less. Solar panels can reduce the use of fossil fuels. Windmills can be used to make electricity. Hybrid cars also use less fuel. If we do not try to be "green," our

planet will soon be in trouble from global warming and the absence of fossil fuels. What kind of world would that be?

The purpose of Elena's paragraph was

A. Narration
B. Entertainment
C. Persuasion
D. Description

60. Students should learn to write for a variety of audiences because

A. Writing everything just for the teacher is boring
B. Their classmates are also a potential audience
C. Students are more involved in their writing if the audience varies
D. Students can make political statements with letters to the editor

61. Which of the following genres takes an opinion and defends it?

A. Essays
B. Biographies
C. Memoirs
D. Informational texts

62. The final resolution of a fictional plot is called

A. Exposition
B. Rising Action
C. Falling Action
D. Denouement

63. Assonance means that two or more words

A. Start with the same sound
B. End with the same sound
C. Have the same vowel sound
D. Sound like an item they portray

64. The basics of writing to a particular audience do NOT include

A. Precise vocabulary
B. Correct facts
C. Figurative language
D. Illustrations or examples

65. The direct instruction model for teaching students to recognize numbers includes

A. Showing newly introduced numbers more often than other numbers
B. Having students count the number of dots and match them to a number
C. Using manipulatives to count and then write a number
D. Showing students the different ways a number can be written

66. Which of the following is an example of an ordinal number?

A. 13
B. One-half
C. Second
D. Ten

67. The property of numbers that states that 1 + 3 is the same as 3 + 1 is called

A. Associative
B. Distributive
C. Inverse
D. Commutative

68. A number system in which the position of a digit in a number determines its value is called a

A. Relationship system
B. Place value system
C. Regrouping system
D. Tens and hundreds system

69. Paper strips and Cuisenaire rods are manipulatives used to teach

A. Place value
B. Fractions
C. Addition of whole numbers
D. Percents

70. A decimal can be converted to a percent by

A. Moving the decimal point two places to the right
B. Dividing by 100
C. Doubling the number
D. Moving the decimal point one place to the left

71. By rewriting 5 times 9 as 9 + 9 +9 + 9 + 9, students will learn

A. The commutative property of numbers
B. The relationship between multiplication and addition
C. The relationship between addition and division
D. The associative property of numbers

72. Although there are 100 addition facts, if students understand commutativity, they actually need to learn

A. 95 facts
B. 75 facts
C. 65 facts
D. 55 facts

73. Which of the following is NOT a model that helps students understand subtraction?

A. Take away
B. Missing addend
C. Number line
D. Adding zero

74. Which of the following is NOT a way to teach young children to recognize patterns?

A. Count by twos beginning with 5
B. Comparing geometric shapes
C. Solving for x in an equation
D. Analyzing the results of a class survey

75. Geometric figures can be classified by

A. The number of sides
B. The angles where sides meet
C. Whether they are polygons or solids
D. All of the above

76. John drew two triangles on a piece of paper, like this:

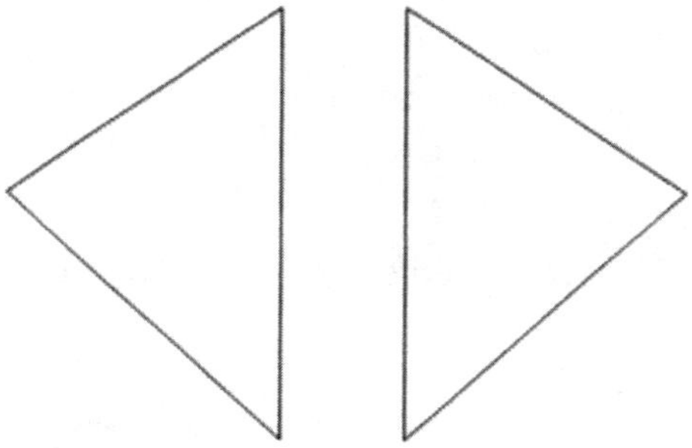

They were facing away from each other, but had the exact same size and shape. This is best described as an example of which geometrical concept?

A. Rotation
B. Reflection
C. Translation
D. Magnification

77. A missing object problem like the one below is one way of helping students learn what concept?
Truck car bike train truck car bike _______ truck car bike train

A. Counting
B. Problem solving
C. Manipulation of objects
D. Basic addition

78. When deciding to measure the sides of a two-dimensional object, what attributes of that object should be considered?

A. Volume and liquid measurement
B. Length and width
C. Weight and mass
D. Perimeter and area

79. What is the educational purpose of having students measure the length of an object, such as their desk or table, with non-standard measuring units smaller than the object, such as crayons?

A. Measuring with small units is easier for young children
B. Children cannot read the markings on a standard ruler or yard stick
C. Students learn to measure something larger than a unit with repetitive use of that unit
D. Students will later be able to transfer measurements from meters to yards

80. For three days, Mr. Hanson had his students keep track of how many times each of them used a pencil during the school day. What is the best kind of graph to use to display these data?

A. Bar graph
B. Circle graph
C. Pictograph
D. Line graph

81. Katrina wanted to solve this math problem: "If there are 30 days in a month and today is the 12th, how many days until the end of the month?" What should be her first problem-solving step?

A. Devise a plan for solving the problem
B. Carry out the plan she created
C. Look back to check that her answer is correct
D. Understand what the problem is asking

82. A third-grade teacher decides to introduce new vocabulary words using a word association game. What is required in order for the students to succeed with word associations?

A. The definition of the new words.
B. Prior knowledge.
C. The spelling of the word.
D. Synonyms of the new words.

83. Which teaching strategy would be best for teaching multiplication tables to a second-grade class?

A. Priming.
B. Discussion.
C. Repetition.
D. Listening.

84. What is a primary contribution of the Israelites to civilization?

A. Secularism
B. Democracy
C. Monarchism
D. Monotheism

85. A major scientific development that began near the beginning of the 17th century was

A. The development of scientific theories
B. The use of experiments to verify theories
C. The concept of an attraction between bodies called gravity
D. The theory of relativity

86. The results of increased production of crops and a managed approach to agriculture is called

A. The industrial revolution
B. The information revolution
C. The agricultural revolution
D. The scientific revolution

87. Which of these refers to the oceans and water areas of earth?

A. Atmosphere
B. Hydrosphere
C. Exosphere
D. Lithosphere

88. What is one benefit of a cooperative learning group?

A. Increased engagement.
B. Socialization.
C. Down time for the teacher.
D. Assistance for struggling students.

89. Due process means

A. It's important for every citizen to follow the laws of their state and country
B. Any accused person may confront the accuser and provide a defense
C. Capital punishment is appropriate if a person is convicted of murder
D. An accused person is considered guilty until proven to be innocent

90. In the Constitution of the United States, which of the following powers are reserved for the states?

A. Taxation
B. Declaring war
C. Regulation of intrastate trade
D. Granting patents and copyrights

91. A law proposed in Congress but not yet passed is called

A. A bill
B. A proposal
C. An introduced law
D. A debate

92. It is snack time in your kindergarten class, and you pour two children equal amounts of water; however, one child's cup is bigger. The child with the bigger cup complains that he has less water. In terms of cognitive development, what can you determine by this complaint?

A. The child has a developmental delay because he does not understand conservation.
B. The child has not reached the concrete operational stage and does not understand conservation; this is normal for a child of this age.
C. The child is displaying a delay in intuitive processes commonly acquired during the pre-operational stage of cognitive development.
D. The child is displaying a preconceptual process that is common among this age group.

93. A belief or opinion in opposition to certain beliefs is called

A. Respect
B. Obedience
C. Dissent
D. Rights

94. Repetition is important to scientific inquiry because

A. It is the only way to prove that an experiment is valid
B. It adds to the number of statistics supporting the concept
C. It assists the scientist in determining which data to consider
D. It requires many groups of investigators working on a project

95. The father of microscopy was

A. Pasteur
B. Koch
C. Leeuwenhoek
D. Watson

96. What effect does science have on technology?

A. Science verifies what technology discovers
B. Technology often results from scientific discoveries
C. Science has no effect on technology; each is independent of the other
D. Scientific progress is dependent on technology

97. Which of the following are required by all organisms in order to survive?

A. Water, cells, shelter, and space
B. Food, water, cellular growth, nurturing
C. Food, water, sunlight, and air
D. Air, shelter, space, and companionship

98. What is the difference between mass and weight?

A. There is no difference; they are the same
B. Mass is the amount of matter in an object; weight is the pull of gravity on the object
C. Mass determines the amount of volume of an object; weight does not
D. Mass is the amount of cubic space that an object occupies. Cubic space is not related to weight

99. World weather patterns are very much influenced by

A. Wind belts
B. The Earth's orbit
C. Ocean currents
D. Atmospheric conditions

100. In the technological design process, after the problem has been identified and a possible solution selected, what is the next step?

A. Propose designs
B. Evaluate the solution
C. Try out the proposed solution
D. Report results

101. What steps should precede drawing a conclusion about a hypothesis?

A. Testing, observing, and recording data
B. Communicating the hypothesis to others
C. Comparing data with data of other groups
D. Writing the results so they can be replicated

Constructed Response

1. Brandon is a five-year-old child who is experiencing typical development in all domains.

- Describe two developmental characteristics that Brandon is most likely exhibiting.
- Explain how the characteristics you described are likely to affect Brandon's learning.

2. Part A: A new student and her parents will be coming into your kindergarten classroom before she begins attending your school. List FOUR materials that they would see in a learning center that will promote visual and auditory skills related to reading.

Part B: As the child is exploring the other learning centers of the classroom, how would you explain to the parents how each of these chosen materials will foster a child's visual and auditory skills related to reading based on principles of child development and learning?

3. A first grade teacher plans to read aloud *Frog and Toad Together*, a story by Arnold Lobel. In the story, Frog and Toad struggle with the temptation to eat too many cookies. The passage below describes what happens.

<u>Cookies</u>

Toad baked some cookies. "These cookies smell very good," said Toad. He ate one. "And they taste even better," he said.

Toad ran to Frog's house. "Frog, Frog," cried Toad, "taste these cookies that I have made."

Frog ate one of the cookies. "These are the best cookies I have ever eaten!" said Frog.

Frog and Toad ate many cookies, one after another. "You know," said Frog, with his mouth full, "I think we should stop eating. We will soon be sick."

"You are right," said Toad. "Let us eat one last cookie, and then we will stop."

Frog and Toad ate one last cookie.

There were many cookies left in the bowl.

"Frog," said Toad, "let us eat one very last cookie, and then we will stop."

Frog and Toad ate one very last cookie.

"We must stop eating!" cried Toad as he ate another.

"Yes," said Frog, reaching for a cookie, "we will need will power."

"What is will power?" asked Toad.

"Will power is trying hard *not* to do something that you really want to do." said Frog.

"You mean like trying *not* to eat all of these cookies?" asked Toad.

"Right," said Frog.

Frog put the cookies in a box.

"There," he said. "Now we will not eat any more cookies."

"But, we can open the box," said Toad.

"That is true," said Frog.

Frog tied some string around the box.

"There," he said. "Now we will not eat any more cookies."

"We can cut the string and open the box," said Toad.

"That is true," said Frog.

Frog got a ladder.

He put the box up on a high shelf.

"There! Now we will not eat any more cookies."

"But, we can climb the ladder, and take the box down from the shelf, and cut the string, and open the box," said Toad.

"That is true," said Frog.

Frog climbed the ladder and took the box down from the shelf.

He cut the string and opened the box.

Frog took the box outside.

He shouted in a loud voice, "HEY BIRDS, HERE ARE COOKIES!"

Birds came from everywhere.

They picked up all the cookies in their beaks and flew away.

"Now we have no more cookies to eat," said Toad sadly. "Not even one."

"Yes," said Frog, "But, we have lots and lots of will power!"

"You may keep it all, Frog," said Toad. "I am going home now to make a cake."

Using your knowledge of first graders' development of literacy and language, answer both of the following:

- Describe two learning activities related to this excerpt that could be used to promote first graders' language and literacy development, making sure to address at least two of the following areas: reading, writing, listening, speaking.
- Explain why each activity you describe would be effective in promoting students' development in the specified areas.

Answers and Explanations

1. D: Analysis. Compare and Contrast is a higher level of thinking and requires analysis.

2. C: Concrete operational stage. The manipulation of objects in the learning process involves using concrete materials to bridge understanding of abstract concepts.

3. B: Conventional. There is actually a hint to this answer in its name. According to Kohlberg, the stage of development during which children learn conventional behavior—e.g., good behavior—is the Conventional Stage.

4. D: Late childhood. This is not one of Erikson's levels of development.

5. B: Microsystem. The family unit and the classroom unit constitute a small social system, a microsystem.

6. C: The importance of play as a learning activity. Vygotsky pointed out that play is the way children learn cooperation and coordination, among other things.

7. A: Students, teachers, and classmates establish knowledge cooperatively every day. In the Constructivist learning theory, the interactions among students, classmates, and teachers were an important contributor to learning.

8. B: The social interaction of students that aid or inhibit learning. According to these theories, students do not just learn in isolation or in a one-on-one relationship with a teacher. They also learn attitudes toward education from their peers, sometimes positive and sometimes negative.

9. C: Report the crisis situation to school or civil authorities. The situation cannot be ignored, but it needs to be dealt with officially and not by the teacher.

10. B: Cooperate with school administrators and public officials to provide assistance, such as a free lunch program and/or academic assistance. Hungry students are not in a position to learn. The family with limited income may not have introduced their child to as many preschool experiences as other children have had, and placement in a special program may be needed to support the child's progress.

11. D: All of the above. There are many possible explanations for a child having decreased attention in class. All should be analyzed to discover the actual problem.

12. B: Acts of jealousy or aggression toward other children. The emotionally-neglected child often behaves negatively toward other children. He or she may not know another way of gaining attention from classmates.

13. B: Play teaches children cooperation and sharing. Play is one way a child learns to relate to other children in a positive way.

14. D: All of the above. Play provides the child with opportunities to develop hand-eye coordination, develop personal interests, and learn to amuse him or herself when alone.

15. D: All areas of development—physical, social, and cognitive—are interrelated. A teacher who is aware of this may be able to emphasize the most appropriate method of instruction for this particular child.

16. D: Developing skills may give clues for the next stage of instruction a student will need. For example, the teacher may observe a child developing skill with manipulative materials and introduce the child to the next step, moving from manipulative to written materials.

17. C: Schizophrenia. The schizophrenic child often has a flat or agitated expression and may speak incoherently or repetitively.

18. D: All of the above. Students with disabilities are best served by a child-centered approach, help in identifying their own learning needs, and need learning experiences that are structured to be appropriate to their needs.

19. B: Sign of emotional difficulties. When children are upset or disturbed, they often manifest their feelings non-verbally in angry outbursts.

20. D: May be abusing drugs. Children using drugs withdraw from social contact and academic activities.

21. B: Having a diagnosed physical or emotional disability that has been professionally evaluated. The child can then be placed in a program that will meet his or her needs. This process often begins with a recommendation by a teacher or parent, but to receive special education services, the child must first be professionally evaluated.

22. A: Lack of sleep or nutrition. Lacking either of these, a child is unable to focus on classroom instruction and may become agitated easily.

23. C: Four years. A child's speech at age four should be between 75 and 100 percent intelligible to strangers. A parent may be more capable of discerning their child's speech since they are more attuned to their child's speech patterns and should understand between 75 and 100 percent intelligible by the age of 3. One hundred percent phonic development is not solidified until age five, but by age four, a child within normal ranges of speech development should be almost fully intelligible to adults.

24. B: Use in-depth evaluation and early intervention to assist the child with language delays. Research shows that early intervention is highly successful, while a wait-and-see approach just prolongs the delayed language development. Common developmental problems like saying "w" instead of "r" disappear on their own as the child matures and do not need intervention.

25. D: Exaggerated efforts to make friends. The child with emotional problems is likely to withdraw from social interactions and exhibit lower academic performance and aggressive behavior.

26. B: Assign the student an appealing task related to the subject area that requires creativity, research, or in-depth study, such as making a collage or creating a play. Assigning the student to tutor classmates does not assist in the intellectual growth of an academically talented student, and the student is apt to resent such an assignment. The teacher needs to be aware that academically talented students also have special academic needs and continue to challenge them with meaningful assignments.

27. A: Vary instructional pace and content to meet the specific needs of disabled students. Answers B, C, and D would stigmatize the disabled student and probably not result in a proper pace and content level.

28. D: The students' classroom teacher. Often, disabilities are not apparent in the home setting, and community agencies will not discover disabled children until informed about them, usually by the teacher.

29. B: Parents know their children's needs, and an IEP must be tailored to meet those needs. The classroom teacher will also be aware of some of those needs, but the child spends more time at home than at school, and the parents may be aware of a disability that is not evident in the classroom but needs to be addressed. Also, the implementation of an IEP is most successful when parents, the school, and the community work together as a team.

30. C: Students with disabilities must be educated in an environment appropriate to them and their non-disabled peers, often a regular classroom. Students with disabilities were formerly segregated into special classes, but the least restrictive environment frequently turns out to be a regular classroom, sometimes with additional assistance for the teacher and the student.

31. D: Assisting students in ways beyond what the classroom teacher can provide. This may include any or all of the assistance suggested in the other answers, such as tutoring, counseling, and assisting or advising parents.

32. A: Focuses on helping emotionally or physically disabled students within the classroom. This is the focus of a 504. An IEP has broader applications to other disabilities or special needs.

33. D: The child's behavior is so difficult that the teacher wants the parents to withdraw the child from school. The teacher may desire this, but has no authority to request it from parents. Sometimes a student will attend school for a limited part of the day, but the decision to limit the day or exclude the child will be made by a team, not by the teacher alone in the process of a teacher-parent conference. Conferences are beneficial for sharing information between a teacher and parents and for enlisting parental support for planned activities involving the child.

34. C: These organizations provide opportunities for children to develop leadership skills and learn to appreciate the value of collaborative processes. Not all community resources are directed toward the disabled child. These organizations, ASB and PTSA, are designed to teach leadership skills to students who show leadership potential. Sometimes a student representative is assigned to the school board for the same reasons.

35. A: Alphabet books, wordless picture books, and easy-to-read books. The other genres are more suitable for older children with well-developed reading skills.

36. D: Instruct students in sciences, such as mathematics and biology. Textbooks have that goal. Children's literature is designed to enhance moral values, instruct through entertaining stories, and promote a life-long interest in reading.

37. B: Fantasy. Fantasy stories and books revolve around magical or supernatural creatures. The Harry Potter books are one example of this genre. Science fiction is a similar genre, but relies on the portrayal of a future world, creatures from other planets or galaxies, etc. Action and Adventure involves solving mysteries. Historical fiction stories are set sometime in the past and are usually accurate in their historical information.

38. A: Action and Adventure. One example of this genre is Nancy Drew. Action and Adventure stories do not rely on magical or supernatural events as do Fantasy, Horror, and Ghost stories. They are not biographical unless telling the life of a real person.

39. A: Simile. The statement is not a metaphor because it contains the word "like." A metaphor does not. An example of a metaphor would be "He was a frozen statue, motionless beside the door." There is no symbolism in the statement, "He ran away like a startled rabbit," nor is there any repetition.

40. B: The ability to understand the abstract concept expressed in metaphors is not developed until later in childhood. Analogies are easier for children to understand because they compare known items, whereas metaphors require abstract thinking.

41. C: In addition to plot, character, setting, and theme, a nonfictional work will also introduce interpretations, theories, and research. For example, a biography is a type of nonfiction that may have plot, character, setting, and theme, and in addition it will introduce interpretations and theories (of the person's life and actions) as well as evidence of the author's research.

42. A: How to tell fiction from nonfiction. This is a skill that children learn by following clues within the literature that point out whether the story is true or not. Young children are not yet ready to distinguish bias in an author's writing or understand themes and theories.

43. C: Class composition and preferences. Before selecting literature for the classroom, the teacher needs to assess the class, considering where they are with their reading skills and what their current interests are. After determining these things, the teacher would next evaluate books that seem appropriate for this particular group of children in terms of plot, character, and reading level.

44. D: Provide a wide variety of reading materials for children to choose from. Each classroom will have students who are just beginning to read and some that are reading fluently above grade level. Providing reading materials with an appealing variety of subject matter and broad distribution of reading levels will ensure that every child in the class can select an appropriate book to read.

45. A: Characters. Children enjoy identifying with a character and experiencing life from that character's point of view. If readers do not bond with a character, they will not enjoy the story.

46. D: All of the above. It is not realistic to expect a teacher to preview every book selected for the classroom, and fortunately there are alternatives, such as asking for help from the school librarian, reading professional reviews, and discussing favorite books with children.

47. C: Style. An author writing a humorous book will use a different style than an author writing a biography.

48. B: Point of view. The point of view is generally first or third person. Stories in the second person exist, but these are rare.

49. A: The *Wild Whale Watch*, part of the Magic School bus series, a chapter book about whales. First graders love to listen to chapter books, but most first graders are not quite able to read chapter books on their own. The undersea fictional adventures in this book will impart a great deal of marine information while simultaneously capturing students' attention with the story. The *Whale Watchers Guide* is not a good choice since the class is not planning a whale watching trip. *Moby Dick* is a well-known adult book, which first graders would not understand. *The Pacific Ocean* will probably offer a lot of marine information, but may not capture first graders' interests.

50. A: In role playing writing, the child writes in scribbles that are only meaningful to him or her. In early writing, the child begins to use real letters.

51. C: Small muscle control. Small muscles are those that enable us to make precise motions, such as gripping a pencil and writing letters with it. Large muscle control involves activities such as running or jumping. The ability to speak is not a developmental skill leading to the ability to write.

52. D: Write thoughts and ideas without stopping to edit them. Freewriting is a prewriting strategy that asks the writer to simply write without any internal editing or concern about formalities, such as spelling or punctuation. The purpose of freewriting is to get the flow of ideas going.

53. D: Organizing writing into paragraphs is done either during the writing process or afterwards in the revision stage. It is not a prewriting strategy.

54. A: In the organization stage of writing, the writer determines the purpose, thesis, and supporting details of the written work. In other words, the organization stage is the part of the writing process where the writer decides on the structure of the proposed written work. In this stage, the writer organizes the ideas already decided upon in the prewriting stage.

55. B: "First we decide who is going to host the holiday dinner." A clue is found in the word "first." A list of actions or ideas often follows a topic sentence.

56. B: It should be written last. Although it is the first part of the written piece, the introduction needs to discuss what is in the entire piece. Until the writing is complete, the writer cannot do that. Writing the introduction first runs the risk that what follows may not completely conform to the ideas expressed in the introduction.

57. D: Students decide whether another student's essay is good writing or poor writing. Peer editing should consist of suggestions for improvement and never involve judgmental decisions about quality.

58. B: Small words in titles like "the" and "of." State names, proper names, and main words in titles should all be capitalized.

59. C: Persuasion. Elena's paragraph was written to persuade. Clues to her purpose can be found in the first and last sentences, which clearly try to influence the reader.

60. C: Students are more involved in their writing if the audience varies. Examples of varied audiences include letters to the editor, letters to a friend, an essay written for a community group, and a story written for younger children or beginning readers.

61. A: Essays. In an essay, the writer defends an opinion, giving reasons for that opinion. Biographies are written to narrate the life of a person. Memoirs detail a person's own life and do not defend opinions. Informational texts are factual.

62. D: Denouement. The denouement is the end of the story. The other choices are intermediate steps in writing a story.

63. C: Have the same vowel sound. Words with assonance have the same vowel sound. An example would be cow and loud.

64. B: Correct and accurate facts are not part of the basics of writing to a particular audience. Some writing for some audiences will not be factual at all, for example, a fairy tale written for young children. The basics of writing to a particular audience include precise vocabulary, figurative language, and illustrations or examples.

65. A: Showing newly introduced numbers more often than other numbers. The direct instruction method depends on repetition of newly introduced numbers. Other methods involve counting dots, using manipulatives, and examining different ways of writing a number.

66. C: Second. Ordinal numbers are first, second, third, fourth, etc.

67. D: Commutative. The property that states that the order in which numbers are added does not change the answer is called the commutative property.

68. B: A place value system. That is the system that requires the position of a digit in a number to determine the digit's value. For example, in the number 123, the digit two is in ten's place, and its value is 20.

69. B: Fractions. Students can manipulate the different lengths of materials like paper strips and Cuisenaire rods, in order to determine that one rod is one half the length of the other, for example.

70. A: Moving the decimal point two places to the right. For example, the decimal 3.42 stands for 342.0 percent of something.

71. B: The relationship between multiplication and addition. By performing these activities, students will see that multiplication is just the repetitive addition of a number a certain number of times.

72. D: 55 facts. When students learn that 3 + 8 is 11, they are also learning that 8 + 3 is 11, so they do not need to memorize 100 facts, just 55.

73. D: Adding zero. Adding zero does not assist students in understanding subtraction. Physically taking some objects away from an array of objects, working a problem with a missing addend like 7 + ___ = 13 helps students learn that 13-7 = 6. Moving to the left on a number line is another way of helping students understand subtraction.

74. C: Solving for x in an equation. Young children are not ready for algebraic equations, but they can learn to recognize patterns by counting by twos, comparing geometric shapes, and analyzing data they have collected.

75. D: All of the above. Geometric figures can be classified in a number of ways, including the number of sides, the angles where sides meet, and as polygons or solids.

76. B: Reflection. One triangle faces the other. They are alike in all other ways. In a rotation, two like figures are rotated about a central point. A translation is a change in the position of a geometric figure. Magnification refers to a change in size of the figure.

77. B: Problem solving. Because an item is missing in the middle of the pattern, the process asked for cannot be counting or addition. Solving this puzzle does not involve manipulation of objects.

78. B: Length and width. Since the object is not a solid, no other dimensions are needed.

79. C: Students learn to measure something larger than a unit by repetitive use of that unit.

80. A: Bar graph. A bar graph is used to compare quantities. A circle is used to compare parts of a whole. A pictograph shows comparison of quantities using symbols. A line graph shows trends over a period of time.

81. D: Understand what the problem is asking. Before you can solve a problem, you must decide what it is about.

82. B: Word associations require a student to pull from previous knowledge or experience. For example, if the student is presented with the word "aardvark" but has never seen or heard of an aardvark, he or she will not be able to make associations. While word association may be a good activity for students after they have reviewed the vocabulary words, it may be counterproductive if the students are unfamiliar with the words. Teachers should also be mindful of cultural differences that may account for a variation in previous knowledge.

83. C: Learning multiplication tables is best accomplished with repetition. As the students repeat the problems and their solutions, connections are made in the brain, and learning is enhanced. While there are many newer methods of teaching and learning, repetition is still useful for a number of tasks. This strategy is also typically used with students learning the alphabet or their phone number and address. Teachers should be aware that young children have short attention spans and can easily become distracted. Therefore, when using repetition as a teaching strategy, the sessions should be relatively short.

84. D: Monotheism. Before the Israelites, almost all civilizations, including the Egyptian, Greek, and Roman civilizations, believed in many gods.

85. B: The use of experiments to verify theories. Before the idea of experimenting was developed, many scientists had theories, often in conflict with each other, but these ideas were never verified scientifically to demonstrate which one was correct. Experiments provided a way to prove ideas.

86. C: The agricultural revolution. A dependable food supply is essential to all populations. The agricultural revolution, an organized, almost scientific approach to agriculture, increased the food supply necessary for a growing world population.

87. B: Hydrosphere. The earth's environment consists of the atmosphere, (the air we breathe), the hydrosphere (water), and the lithosphere (the land).

88. A: In the classroom setting, some students may be hesitant to openly participate. This may be due to a number of reasons, including the fear of being wrong or shyness. Utilizing cooperative learning groups is one way to increase student participation in class. Creating smaller groups within the class allows students to participate in a less threatening environment. Additionally, motivation and overall outcomes have also been shown to improve in these environments. Using these learning groups in conjunction with other teaching methods keeps students interested and engaged.

89. B: The right of a defendant to confront accusers and to provide a defense.

90. C: Regulate intrastate trade. Intrastate trade is solely within a state, so the state has jurisdiction over it. Taxation is a right granted to both federal and state authorities. Declaring war is a national decision. Patents and copyrights apply to goods made and/or sold throughout the country; therefore, they are a federal responsibility.

91. A: A bill. A bill is a proposed law.

92. B: The child is developing normally; typical of his age group, he is in the preoperational stage of development and has not yet mastered conservation. Conservation is the ability to use logical reasoning to determine quantity. In this case, the child thinks one glass has more water simply

because the glass is bigger. As this child enters into the concrete operational stage of development, he will understand that two amounts can be equal despite the size or shape of the container they are in. However, since this skill is not yet developed, the child will continue to believe one has more. If the teacher pours the water from the bigger glass into a glass that equals the size of his classmate's, the child will have a different reaction and possibly think the two are now equal.

93. C: Dissent. Dissent occurs when a citizen disagrees with a certain concept or law.

94. A: It is the only way to prove that an experiment is valid. If an experiment can't be successfully repeated with the same outcome, one cannot determine that the experimental results are valid. Repetition is the key to scientific progress.

95. C: Leeuwenhoek. Pasteur discovered the role of micro-organisms in disease. Koch determined that each disease has a specific pathogen. James Watson developed the science of genetics.

96. B: Technology often results from scientific discoveries. The relationship between science and technology is evident when scientific discoveries prompt technologic advances.

97. C: Food, water, sunlight, and air. All living organisms need food, water, sunlight and air. Shelter, space, and nurturing are nice to have but not crucial to sustaining life.

98. B: Mass. Mass is the amount of matter in an object. Weight is the measure of the pull of gravity on an object.

99. C: Ocean currents. Wind belts, the Earth's orbit, and atmospheric conditions have some effect on weather, but ocean currents have the greatest influence.

100. C: Try out the proposed solution. The first step is to identify a problem and propose a solution. Trying the solution comes next, followed by evaluation and reporting the results.

101. A: Testing, observing, and recording data. Before drawing a conclusion about a hypothesis, one should test and observe it and record data about the test results.

How to Overcome Test Anxiety

Just the thought of taking a test is enough to make most people a little nervous. A test is an important event that can have a long-term impact on your future, so it's important to take it seriously and it's natural to feel anxious about performing well. But just because anxiety is normal, that doesn't mean that it's helpful in test taking, or that you should simply accept it as part of your life. Anxiety can have a variety of effects. These effects can be mild, like making you feel slightly nervous, or severe, like blocking your ability to focus or remember even a simple detail.

If you experience test anxiety—whether severe or mild—it's important to know how to beat it. To discover this, first you need to understand what causes test anxiety.

Causes of Test Anxiety

While we often think of anxiety as an uncontrollable emotional state, it can actually be caused by simple, practical things. One of the most common causes of test anxiety is that a person does not feel adequately prepared for their test. This feeling can be the result of many different issues such as poor study habits or lack of organization, but the most common culprit is time management. Starting to study too late, failing to organize your study time to cover all of the material, or being distracted while you study will mean that you're not well prepared for the test. This may lead to cramming the night before, which will cause you to be physically and mentally exhausted for the test. Poor time management also contributes to feelings of stress, fear, and hopelessness as you realize you are not well prepared but don't know what to do about it.

Other times, test anxiety is not related to your preparation for the test but comes from unresolved fear. This may be a past failure on a test, or poor performance on tests in general. It may come from comparing yourself to others who seem to be performing better or from the stress of living up to expectations. Anxiety may be driven by fears of the future—how failure on this test would affect your educational and career goals. These fears are often completely irrational, but they can still negatively impact your test performance.

Review Video: 3 Reasons You Have Test Anxiety
Visit mometrix.com/academy and enter code: 428468

Elements of Test Anxiety

As mentioned earlier, test anxiety is considered to be an emotional state, but it has physical and mental components as well. Sometimes you may not even realize that you are suffering from test anxiety until you notice the physical symptoms. These can include trembling hands, rapid heartbeat, sweating, nausea, and tense muscles. Extreme anxiety may lead to fainting or vomiting. Obviously, any of these symptoms can have a negative impact on testing. It is important to recognize them as soon as they begin to occur so that you can address the problem before it damages your performance.

Review Video: 3 Ways to Tell You Have Test Anxiety
Visit mometrix.com/academy and enter code: 927847

The mental components of test anxiety include trouble focusing and inability to remember learned information. During a test, your mind is on high alert, which can help you recall information and stay focused for an extended period of time. However, anxiety interferes with your mind's natural processes, causing you to blank out, even on the questions you know well. The strain of testing during anxiety makes it difficult to stay focused, especially on a test that may take several hours. Extreme anxiety can take a huge mental toll, making it difficult not only to recall test information but even to understand the test questions or pull your thoughts together.

Review Video: How Test Anxiety Affects Memory
Visit mometrix.com/academy and enter code: 609003

Effects of Test Anxiety

Test anxiety is like a disease—if left untreated, it will get progressively worse. Anxiety leads to poor performance, and this reinforces the feelings of fear and failure, which in turn lead to poor performances on subsequent tests. It can grow from a mild nervousness to a crippling condition. If allowed to progress, test anxiety can have a big impact on your schooling, and consequently on your future.

Test anxiety can spread to other parts of your life. Anxiety on tests can become anxiety in any stressful situation, and blanking on a test can turn into panicking in a job situation. But fortunately, you don't have to let anxiety rule your testing and determine your grades. There are a number of relatively simple steps you can take to move past anxiety and function normally on a test and in the rest of life.

Review Video: How Test Anxiety Impacts Your Grades
Visit mometrix.com/academy and enter code: 939819

Physical Steps for Beating Test Anxiety

While test anxiety is a serious problem, the good news is that it can be overcome. It doesn't have to control your ability to think and remember information. While it may take time, you can begin taking steps today to beat anxiety.

Just as your first hint that you may be struggling with anxiety comes from the physical symptoms, the first step to treating it is also physical. Rest is crucial for having a clear, strong mind. If you are tired, it is much easier to give in to anxiety. But if you establish good sleep habits, your body and mind will be ready to perform optimally, without the strain of exhaustion. Additionally, sleeping well helps you to retain information better, so you're more likely to recall the answers when you see the test questions.

Getting good sleep means more than going to bed on time. It's important to allow your brain time to relax. Take study breaks from time to time so it doesn't get overworked, and don't study right before bed. Take time to rest your mind before trying to rest your body, or you may find it difficult to fall asleep.

Review Video: The Importance of Sleep for Your Brain
Visit mometrix.com/academy and enter code: 319338

Along with sleep, other aspects of physical health are important in preparing for a test. Good nutrition is vital for good brain function. Sugary foods and drinks may give a burst of energy but this burst is followed by a crash, both physically and emotionally. Instead, fuel your body with protein and vitamin-rich foods.

Also, drink plenty of water. Dehydration can lead to headaches and exhaustion, especially if your brain is already under stress from the rigors of the test. Particularly if your test is a long one, drink water during the breaks. And if possible, take an energy-boosting snack to eat between sections.

Review Video: How Diet Can Affect your Mood
Visit mometrix.com/academy and enter code: 624317

Along with sleep and diet, a third important part of physical health is exercise. Maintaining a steady workout schedule is helpful, but even taking 5-minute study breaks to walk can help get your blood pumping faster and clear your head. Exercise also releases endorphins, which contribute to a positive feeling and can help combat test anxiety.

When you nurture your physical health, you are also contributing to your mental health. If your body is healthy, your mind is much more likely to be healthy as well. So take time to rest, nourish your body with healthy food and water, and get moving as much as possible. Taking these physical steps will make you stronger and more able to take the mental steps necessary to overcome test anxiety.

Review Video: How to Stay Healthy and Prevent Test Anxiety
Visit mometrix.com/academy and enter code: 877894

Mental Steps for Beating Test Anxiety

Working on the mental side of test anxiety can be more challenging, but as with the physical side, there are clear steps you can take to overcome it. As mentioned earlier, test anxiety often stems from lack of preparation, so the obvious solution is to prepare for the test. Effective studying may be the most important weapon you have for beating test anxiety, but you can and should employ several other mental tools to combat fear.

First, boost your confidence by reminding yourself of past success—tests or projects that you aced. If you're putting as much effort into preparing for this test as you did for those, there's no reason you should expect to fail here. Work hard to prepare; then trust your preparation.

Second, surround yourself with encouraging people. It can be helpful to find a study group, but be sure that the people you're around will encourage a positive attitude. If you spend time with others who are anxious or cynical, this will only contribute to your own anxiety. Look for others who are motivated to study hard from a desire to succeed, not from a fear of failure.

Third, reward yourself. A test is physically and mentally tiring, even without anxiety, and it can be helpful to have something to look forward to. Plan an activity following the test, regardless of the outcome, such as going to a movie or getting ice cream.

When you are taking the test, if you find yourself beginning to feel anxious, remind yourself that you know the material. Visualize successfully completing the test. Then take a few deep, relaxing breaths and return to it. Work through the questions carefully but with confidence, knowing that you are capable of succeeding.

Developing a healthy mental approach to test taking will also aid in other areas of life. Test anxiety affects more than just the actual test—it can be damaging to your mental health and even contribute to depression. It's important to beat test anxiety before it becomes a problem for more than testing.

Review Video: Test Anxiety and Depression
Visit mometrix.com/academy and enter code: 904704

Study Strategy

Being prepared for the test is necessary to combat anxiety, but what does being prepared look like? You may study for hours on end and still not feel prepared. What you need is a strategy for test prep. The next few pages outline our recommended steps to help you plan out and conquer the challenge of preparation.

Step 1: Scope Out the Test

Learn everything you can about the format (multiple choice, essay, etc.) and what will be on the test. Gather any study materials, course outlines, or sample exams that may be available. Not only will this help you to prepare, but knowing what to expect can help to alleviate test anxiety.

Step 2: Map Out the Material

Look through the textbook or study guide and make note of how many chapters or sections it has. Then divide these over the time you have. For example, if a book has 15 chapters and you have five days to study, you need to cover three chapters each day. Even better, if you have the time, leave an extra day at the end for overall review after you have gone through the material in depth.

If time is limited, you may need to prioritize the material. Look through it and make note of which sections you think you already have a good grasp on, and which need review. While you are studying, skim quickly through the familiar sections and take more time on the challenging parts. Write out your plan so you don't get lost as you go. Having a written plan also helps you feel more in control of the study, so anxiety is less likely to arise from feeling overwhelmed at the amount to cover. A sample plan may look like this:

- Day 1: Skim chapters 1–4, study chapter 5 (especially pages 31–33)
- Day 2: Study chapters 6–7, skim chapters 8–9
- Day 3: Skim chapter 10, study chapters 11–12 (especially pages 87–90)
- Day 4: Study chapters 13–15
- Day 5: Overall review (focus most on chapters 5, 6, and 12), take practice test

Step 3: Gather Your Tools

Decide what study method works best for you. Do you prefer to highlight in the book as you study and then go back over the highlighted portions? Or do you type out notes of the important information? Or is it helpful to make flashcards that you can carry with you? Assemble the pens, index cards, highlighters, post-it notes, and any other materials you may need so you won't be distracted by getting up to find things while you study.

If you're having a hard time retaining the information or organizing your notes, experiment with different methods. For example, try color-coding by subject with colored pens, highlighters, or post-it notes. If you learn better by hearing, try recording yourself reading your notes so you can listen while in the car, working out, or simply sitting at your desk. Ask a friend to quiz you from your flashcards, or try teaching someone the material to solidify it in your mind.

Step 4: Create Your Environment

It's important to avoid distractions while you study. This includes both the obvious distractions like visitors and the subtle distractions like an uncomfortable chair (or a too-comfortable couch that makes you want to fall asleep). Set up the best study environment possible: good lighting and a comfortable work area. If background music helps you focus, you may want to turn it on, but otherwise keep the room quiet. If you are using a computer to take notes, be sure you don't have any other windows open, especially applications like social media, games, or anything else that could distract you. Silence your phone and turn off notifications. Be sure to keep water close by so you stay hydrated while you study (but avoid unhealthy drinks and snacks).

Also, take into account the best time of day to study. Are you freshest first thing in the morning? Try to set aside some time then to work through the material. Is your mind clearer in the afternoon or evening? Schedule your study session then. Another method is to study at the same time of day that you will take the test, so that your brain gets used to working on the material at that time and will be ready to focus at test time.

Step 5: Study!

Once you have done all the study preparation, it's time to settle into the actual studying. Sit down, take a few moments to settle your mind so you can focus, and begin to follow your study plan. Don't give in to distractions or let yourself procrastinate. This is your time to prepare so you'll be ready to fearlessly approach the test. Make the most of the time and stay focused.

Of course, you don't want to burn out. If you study too long you may find that you're not retaining the information very well. Take regular study breaks. For example, taking five minutes out of every hour to walk briskly, breathing deeply and swinging your arms, can help your mind stay fresh.

As you get to the end of each chapter or section, it's a good idea to do a quick review. Remind yourself of what you learned and work on any difficult parts. When you feel that you've mastered the material, move on to the next part. At the end of your study session, briefly skim through your notes again.

But while review is helpful, cramming last minute is NOT. If at all possible, work ahead so that you won't need to fit all your study into the last day. Cramming overloads your brain with more information than it can process and retain, and your tired mind may struggle to recall even previously learned information when it is overwhelmed with last-minute study. Also, the urgent nature of cramming and the stress placed on your brain contribute to anxiety. You'll be more likely to go to the test feeling unprepared and having trouble thinking clearly.

So don't cram, and don't stay up late before the test, even just to review your notes at a leisurely pace. Your brain needs rest more than it needs to go over the information again. In fact, plan to finish your studies by noon or early afternoon the day before the test. Give your brain the rest of the day to relax or focus on other things, and get a good night's sleep. Then you will be fresh for the test and better able to recall what you've studied.

Step 6: Take a practice test

Many courses offer sample tests, either online or in the study materials. This is an excellent resource to check whether you have mastered the material, as well as to prepare for the test format and environment.

Check the test format ahead of time: the number of questions, the type (multiple choice, free response, etc.), and the time limit. Then create a plan for working through them. For example, if you have 30 minutes to take a 60-question test, your limit is 30 seconds per question. Spend less time on the questions you know well so that you can take more time on the difficult ones.

If you have time to take several practice tests, take the first one open book, with no time limit. Work through the questions at your own pace and make sure you fully understand them. Gradually work up to taking a test under test conditions: sit at a desk with all study materials put away and set a timer. Pace yourself to make sure you finish the test with time to spare and go back to check your answers if you have time.

After each test, check your answers. On the questions you missed, be sure you understand why you missed them. Did you misread the question (tests can use tricky wording)? Did you forget the information? Or was it something you hadn't learned? Go back and study any shaky areas that the practice tests reveal.

Taking these tests not only helps with your grade, but also aids in combating test anxiety. If you're already used to the test conditions, you're less likely to worry about it, and working through tests until you're scoring well gives you a confidence boost. Go through the practice tests until you feel comfortable, and then you can go into the test knowing that you're ready for it.

Test Tips

On test day, you should be confident, knowing that you've prepared well and are ready to answer the questions. But aside from preparation, there are several test day strategies you can employ to maximize your performance.

First, as stated before, get a good night's sleep the night before the test (and for several nights before that, if possible). Go into the test with a fresh, alert mind rather than staying up late to study.

Try not to change too much about your normal routine on the day of the test. It's important to eat a nutritious breakfast, but if you normally don't eat breakfast at all, consider eating just a protein bar. If you're a coffee drinker, go ahead and have your normal coffee. Just make sure you time it so that the caffeine doesn't wear off right in the middle of your test. Avoid sugary beverages, and drink enough water to stay hydrated but not so much that you need a restroom break 10 minutes into the test. If your test isn't first thing in the morning, consider going for a walk or doing a light workout before the test to get your blood flowing.

Allow yourself enough time to get ready, and leave for the test with plenty of time to spare so you won't have the anxiety of scrambling to arrive in time. Another reason to be early is to select a good seat. It's helpful to sit away from doors and windows, which can be distracting. Find a good seat, get out your supplies, and settle your mind before the test begins.

When the test begins, start by going over the instructions carefully, even if you already know what to expect. Make sure you avoid any careless mistakes by following the directions.

Then begin working through the questions, pacing yourself as you've practiced. If you're not sure on an answer, don't spend too much time on it, and don't let it shake your confidence. Either skip it and come back later, or eliminate as many wrong answers as possible and guess among the remaining ones. Don't dwell on these questions as you continue—put them out of your mind and focus on what lies ahead.

Be sure to read all of the answer choices, even if you're sure the first one is the right answer. Sometimes you'll find a better one if you keep reading. But don't second-guess yourself if you do immediately know the answer. Your gut instinct is usually right. Don't let test anxiety rob you of the information you know.

If you have time at the end of the test (and if the test format allows), go back and review your answers. Be cautious about changing any, since your first instinct tends to be correct, but make sure you didn't misread any of the questions or accidentally mark the wrong answer choice. Look over any you skipped and make an educated guess.

At the end, leave the test feeling confident. You've done your best, so don't waste time worrying about your performance or wishing you could change anything. Instead, celebrate the successful completion of this test. And finally, use this test to learn how to deal with anxiety even better next time.

Review Video: 5 Tips to Beat Test Anxiety
Visit mometrix.com/academy and enter code: 570656

Important Qualification

Not all anxiety is created equal. If your test anxiety is causing major issues in your life beyond the classroom or testing center, or if you are experiencing troubling physical symptoms related to your anxiety, it may be a sign of a serious physiological or psychological condition. If this sounds like your situation, we strongly encourage you to seek professional help.

Thank You

We at Mometrix would like to extend our heartfelt thanks to you, our friend and patron, for allowing us to play a part in your journey. It is a privilege to serve people from all walks of life who are unified in their commitment to building the best future they can for themselves.

The preparation you devote to these important testing milestones may be the most valuable educational opportunity you have for making a real difference in your life. We encourage you to put your heart into it—that feeling of succeeding, overcoming, and yes, conquering will be well worth the hours you've invested.

We want to hear your story, your struggles and your successes, and if you see any opportunities for us to improve our materials so we can help others even more effectively in the future, please share that with us as well. **The team at Mometrix would be absolutely thrilled to hear from you!** So please, send us an email (support@mometrix.com) and let's stay in touch.

If you'd like some additional help, check out these other resources we offer for your exam:

http://MometrixFlashcards.com/MEGA

Additional Bonus Material

Due to our efforts to try to keep this book to a manageable length, we've created a link that will give you access to all of your additional bonus material.

Please visit http://www.mometrix.com/bonus948/megaearlyced to access the information.